LIVE

LIKE

JESUS

LIVE

LIKE

JESUS

—

HOW HE CALLS US TO MAKE DISCIPLES

DANN SPADER

MOODY PUBLISHERS
CHICAGO

This book was previously published as *Discipling as Jesus Discipled: 7 Disciplines of a Disciplemaker.*

Edited by Brandon O'Brien
Interior design: Clear Design Group
Cover design: Phil Borst and Dave Rawlins

The Library of Congress has cataloged the first printing of this book as follows:

Names: Spader, Dann, author.
Title: Discipling as Jesus discipled : 7 disciplines of a disciple-maker by
  Dann Spader.
Description: Chicago : Moody Publishers, 2016. | Description based on print
  version record and CIP data provided by publisher; resource not viewed.
Identifiers: LCCN 2016020384 (print) | LCCN 2016019852 (ebook) | ISBN
  9780802495044 () | ISBN 9780802414632
Subjects: LCSH: Discipling (Christianity) | Jesus Christ--Example.
Classification: LCC BV4520 (print) | LCC BV4520 .S6243 2016 (ebook) | DDC
  253--dc23
LC record available at https://lccn.loc.gov/2016020384

ISBN: 978-0-8024-1882-1

Special Thanks:

To my wife Char, my best friend and partner for over thirty-five years;
to our three wonderful daughters: Julie, Jamie, and Christy;
to our two sons-in-law: Pete and Brandon; and to our eight amazing
grandkids: Keira, Kellon, Karsyn, Kamri, Elyse, Shepherd, Hope, and Connor.
Eight of the cutest grandkids anyone could ever have!
Thanks for making our family such a wonderful part of life!

And

To our Neighborhood Missional Community:
You truly are a band of brothers and sisters. Your passion for the Lord
and heart to see His kingdom advanced are inspirational.
Thanks for your friendship and encouragement.
Special thanks to our Neighborhood Ministry Team for living out
these values and letting me live life with you.
Ron and Suzanne Albertsen, Wendy and Billy Brewer, Barry and
Carla Motes, and Mike and Terri Rolfe—your commitment to
impart your life to others is truly doing what Jesus did.

Learn more about the Like Jesus initiative for your church
or ministry and access videos and assessment tools at:
www.LikeJesus.church/live

—

LIKE JESUS

CONTENTS

HOW TO GET THE MOST FROM THIS STUDY

—

Live Like Jesus is a resource for small groups or individuals who have a desire to study the life of Christ and go deeper in understanding how Christ made disciples. Taken from Jesus' own words in John 17, we look at His seven "I" statements and seek to practically apply these to our own lives.

This resource has been designed to be a 10–12 week study, but can be adapted to a longer time frame, depending on the needs and interests of the group. Designed primarily as a small group interactive study, this resource can also be used for personal study or one-on-one discipling. Feel free to use it as best serves your needs or that of your group. A leader's guide is available free at LikeJesus.church/live.

Each session in this book has been designed with an introductory overview called "Getting Started" followed by 4–5 days of personal study to be done prior to the group meeting. Each of these "Days" takes approximately 15–20 minutes to complete. Feel free to mark up your book, adding additional insights or questions you may have as you study the text. Bring any of these questions or insights with you to the small group interaction time. The free online leader's guide will serve as a tool to help the group facilitator guide the group interaction time.

4-Chair
Go to LikeJesus.church/4chair

Walk Like Jesus
Go to LikeJesus.church/walk

Live Like Jesus
Go to LikeJesus.church/live

Our prayer is that you will gain a fresh look at Christ and see in His prayer in John 17 a simple model of what it means to do what Jesus did (John 14:12). Allow the Spirit of God to teach you as you look intently at the Scriptures, and let Him to transform your life. At the end of this study, we have sought to provide a very simple tool of taking what you have learned and applying it to your life as you seek to help others follow Christ, fully living out His character and priorities.

Our mission is very clear. It is to make disciples who can make disciples.

Jesus summarized His life in Matthew 28:16–20, telling us to do what He did (John 14:12) by walking as He walked (1 John 2:6). That mission statement is emphasized in the first command of the Great Commission (reflected by the imperative mood in the Greek text)—"make disciples." As we make disciples, we are given a second imperative in the text: "behold" (v. 20 ESV). This literally means, *Keep your eyes on me as you make disciples.*

"Making disciples" was the core of Jesus' life, and it must become the focus of our lives and the life of our churches.

But to fully understand the mandate to "make disciples," it is helpful to look at the four other great commission statements in the other Gospels and the book of Acts.

Matthew 28 gives us the *method* of making disciples: go, baptize, and teach to obey. This can be simply translated, "*As you go*, do what Jesus did." Become a friend of sinners and share the good news. When your friends repent and believe, "baptiz[e] them" as an expression of their identifying with the work and cause of Christ. Finally "teach[] them to obey" all that He has commanded you, equipping them in every area of their life to walk as Jesus walked. Win the lost, establish the believers, and equip the few workers to reproduce the process. Make disciples who can make disciples.

John gives us the *model* of disciple-making: "As the Father has sent me, I am sending you" (John 20:21). In order to learn how to live out Matthew 28, we need to go back and master the Master's life. He showed us how to create a movement of multiplying disciples.

Mark demonstrates the *magnitude* of our disciple-making priorities: "Go into all the world and preach the gospel to all creation" (Mark 16:15). The mission begins where we live—with our families, our neighbors, and our community—but extends to the whole world.

Luke presents with clarity the *message* of disciples: "repentance for the forgiveness of sins will be preached in his name to all nations, beginning at Jerusalem" (Luke 24:47). Any message that is devoid of repentance and the forgiveness of sins is a faulty gospel.

And finally, Acts gives us the *means* of disciple-making: "But you will receive power when the Holy Spirit comes on you; and you will be my witnesses in Jerusalem, and in all Judea and Samaria, and to the ends of the earth" (Acts 1:8). Just like Jesus, we are fully dependent upon the Spirit's power to achieve this process.

The mission is clear—to make disciples who can make disciples. Each gospel account contributes a different element of the mission. Together they describe one clear goal: to make disciples the way Jesus did.

Live Like Jesus is a study about *disciple-making*, not discipleship. There is a major difference between the two! Discipleship is normally defined as helping believers to grow. Jesus did not command us to "go and do discipleship." He commanded us to "go and make disciples." Disciple-making is the whole process of reaching the lost, building up the new believer, and then equipping the worker to repeat the process in the lives of others. In this study, I will constantly refer to disciple-making as the whole process of being a friend of sinners, helping them find Jesus and follow Him, and then teaching them to go and repeat the process with others.

In my recent book *4 Chair Discipling*, I go into more detail about this process. Using the metaphor of four chairs, I looked at how Jesus masterfully challenged His disciples through a growth process. "Come and see" (John 1:39 KJV) was the first challenge, given for seekers to explore their relationship with Christ. "Follow me" (John 1:43) was the second challenge, given to His disciples to walk in His steps and learn from Him. "Follow me, and I will make you fishers of men" (Matt. 4:19 ESV) was the challenge He gave nearly eighteen months later, calling a few to go deeper in learning how to reproduce their lives in others. And, finally, in His fourth challenge, "go and bear fruit" (John 15:16), Jesus sends out His disciples toward the end of His ministry to repeat the process in others. He made disciples who could make disciples, intentionally developing them through a well-defined and natural process.

"Making disciples" was the core of Jesus' life, and it must become the focus of our lives and the life of our churches. Not only did Jesus clearly command us to "go and make disciples," but it was also the clear focus of His ministry calling. As we study John 17 together, we will see in Jesus' own words how He prioritized His disciples.

Disciple-making Jesus-style was a way of life. Jesus clearly stated, "Follow me, and I will make you fishers of men" (Matt. 4:19 ESV). In this simple challenge, we can see that Jesus' model of discipling was relational: "follow me" (chapter 1); intentional: "I will make you" (chapters 3–9); and missional: "fishers of men" (chapter 10). Jesus' model of discipling involved definite values and priorities, which Jesus modeled in His life. This is the purpose of this study—to dig into the Scriptures to see those values and priorities and seek to emulate them in our own lives. We will use Jesus' own words in John 17 as the baseline for our study.

Throughout this study, I ask different kinds of questions. Some questions are directly related to details in the biblical text. They can be found simply by reading the biblical passage. Other times, the questions are indirectly taken from the text, which means you'll need to think creatively about the concepts presented in the Bible passage. These types of questions require more reflection and, ideally, discussion with others. There are no black-and-white answers. All of these questions are designed to help you think beyond the simple answers as you study God's Word.

Dig deep. Think hard. Discuss this with your friends. Together, let's go further in making disciples like Jesus did. May He use this study in your life and in your disciples' lives as you think deeper about His life and ministry.

RELATIONAL: "COME, FOLLOW ME"

(MATTHEW 4:19A)

Go deeper: Watch videos online and download the Like Jesus app. LikeJesus.church/live

GETTING STARTED

Three words capture how Jesus made disciples: relational, intentional, and missional. These three words come directly from Matthew 4:19 when, eighteen months into His ministry, Jesus approaches James and John and Simon and Andrew (and later on Matthew) and challenges them to go deeper with Him. Having been with some disciples for a year and a half, Jesus is going to move into a player/coach role with His disciples, and these men are His starting five. His challenge will be: "Follow me [relational], and I will make you [intentional] fishers of men [missional]" (ESV). This week we start looking at Jesus' relational method for making disciples.

But before we begin, let me introduce you to Vi.

Vi lived in a Midwestern farming community and attended a small rural church of less than 150 people. Vi loved the Lord and sought to live her life for Him. At a weeklong missions conference in her church, the speaker kept talking about "making disciples" from the Great Commission text of Matthew 28. Vi knew this process began with a willingness to share her faith with her farming neighbors who did not know the Lord.

As Vi struggled to figure out how to embrace the Great Commission in her life, she felt like such a failure. "Lord, I want to please You and do what You have commanded," Vi prayed, "but I'm just not gifted in evangelism." All week Vi wrestled with what she was hearing. Finally, at the end of the week she said, "Okay, God, I will try!"

With her farming neighbors on her mind, Vi prayed for the courage to visit them and share the good news with them. Vi stopped at her neighbor's home, and the woman invited her in and offered her a cup of coffee. As the conversation progressed, Vi managed to turn the discussion toward the gospel. During her presentation of the gospel, the man of the home entered the kitchen. The man listened in on the conversation and became increasingly agitated.

Finally he burst out in anger, "We have our own religion and don't need you selling us yours. You can leave now!"

Vi went home feeling that she had failed God miserably. "God, I know that the first step of making disciples is sharing the good news, but I tried and failed," she told the Lord.

Later that day, as providence would have it, the boy from the farm that she was just kicked off of was playing in her yard with her son. She looked at this young boy and prayed, "Lord, I failed at sharing the gospel, but I can pray! And if you will help me, I will pray every day for that boy to find Christ!"

She set her heart to praying. That young boy went to high school, off to college, and then (through a series of miracles) found Christ at college. He began to share his story with others, leading several young men in his fraternity house and several family members to Christ. One time when that young boy was back on the farm, he heard through the grapevine that Vi knew Jesus.

He went over to Vi's home and asked her, "Do you know Jesus the way I do?"

"What do you mean?" Vi asked.

"Well, about two months ago, my roommate shared Christ with me, and I asked Him into my life. My life has been changed. I'm sharing with others. I'm in a Bible study that is teaching me so much, and God is doing some amazing things. Some of my family is also finding Christ's love and forgiveness. Do you know Jesus that way?" he asked.

Vi started crying.

> Disciple-making is nothing more than sharing the good news of the gospel and seeking to multiply Christ's character and priorities in others through our web of relationships.

"Did I say something wrong?" the boy asked.

"No," Vi said. "I've been praying for you for over ten years!"

All of a sudden that young boy started crying too.

I know that story well, because I was that young boy! On December 17, 1970, I accepted Christ in a fraternity house after a beer party. And I'm convinced that was because Vi prayed for me for more than ten years. To my knowledge, I was the first in my family to accept Christ.

Now many in our family know Jesus personally. Hundreds, if not thousands, have come to Christ because of Vi's prayers. My family has been forever changed, saying nothing about the multiple future generations that have been altered because of Vi's prayers. Her prayers began the process that led to my becoming a disciple of Christ and then later growing in disciple-making.

Disciple-making is nothing more than sharing the good news of the gospel and seeking to multiply Christ's character and priorities in others through our web of relationships. Vi was crucial in the disciple-making process because she was willing to step out by faith and initiate this process in our family. Her prayers for me through the years served as the platform for my coming to faith and then growing in Him.

All disciple-making is relational and thus it begins with us living out that good news within our relationships. Vi understood that God wanted her to begin within her sphere of relationships. And fortunately for me, she obeyed! My life and eternal destiny has been forever changed. Vi looked at her relational network and, because of her love for God and for people, she began there. And today the fruit of her faithfulness continues around the world.

Who first shared with you the good news of the gospel? What kind of relationship did you have with this person? (Was it a family member, neighbor, or friend?)

How well did you receive them when they shared with you the truth of the gospel? What were the major reasons that caused you to believe?

It has often been said that all true life-change comes through relationship—a relationship with friends, family members, work associates, or a relationship with God. Do you agree with this statement? Why or why not?

TAKING THE NEXT STEP:

My Personal Story:

I grew up in a very large Midwestern farm family. When I say it was large, I mean *large.* There were sixteen children in our family, and I was number fifteen of sixteen. We were a very religious family. We went to church every Sunday and prayed before meals.

But when I became a teenager, I turned away from my religious upbringing. My faith was superficial and impersonal. God increasingly became an object to fear, not the personal caring Father that I had been told about as a child. At college, I sought once again to know God personally, but with no success. I soon gave up the search and became consumed with success and the party life. I succeeded in joining the most popular fraternity on campus, was elected class president, and began to run for student body president. But every weekend was the same: go to parties and get drunk, only to regret my actions once the weekend was over.

But then something powerful happened. My roommate, who always joined me at drinking parties, stopped wanting to get drunk. He had attended a Christian conference and heard about biblical repentance and inviting Christ into his life. I noticed a powerful change in his words, actions, and priorities.

One night after a keg party, I came back to our fraternity house, only to find him reading his Bible. I was shocked. "What happened to you?" I asked.

"Do you really want to know?"

"Yes."

He then pulled out a gospel tract called the *Four Spiritual Laws* and began to share with me how much God loved me, how I was separated from God because of my sins, and how I needed to repent of my sin and receive Christ into my life. I clearly remember him sharing with me Revelation 3:20: "Here I am! I stand at the door and knock. If anyone hears my voice and opens the door, I will come in and eat with that person, and they with me."

My roommate asked me if I wanted Christ in my life and if I was willing to turn from my sin. That night, December 17, 1970, I invited Christ into my life as Lord and Savior.

My life has never been the same. Soon after I invited Christ into my life, I found out about Vi praying for me for over ten years. I was discipled by a young man on campus who led my roommate and me into a study of basic Christian truths. Vi also shared with me what she knew of the Lord. We began immediately to share our faith with others. Soon, as others accepted Christ, we realized we needed to help them grow. God quickly gave my life meaning, purpose, and a new sense of direction. I found many new friends who loved the Lord, and we began the exciting journey of being disciples and building other disciples.

How well can you articulate "your story" of coming to Christ? Write out three or four sentences that answer each of these questions in "your story." Share your story with someone else.

1. What was your life like before you accepted Christ?

2. What led you to understand the gospel? How did you accept Christ? (Share some Scripture verses that helped you understand.)

3. What has changed in your life since you accepted Christ? What difference has it made?

DAY ONE

JOHN 13 AND RELATIONAL LIVING

The focus of this study is how Jesus made disciples. Since all Scripture points to Jesus, in reality we could go anywhere in the Bible and learn from Christ. However, we will focus in this study on the earthly life of Christ (Heb. 5:7) that is primarily recorded in the Gospels. This is the life that we are called to imitate (1 John 2:6).

In John 17, we will use the actual words that Jesus used to describe what He did with His disciples. These are the seven disciplines of a disciple-maker. They are seven "I" statements:

> Verse 6 (see also v. 26): "I have revealed you to those whom you gave me"
>
> Verse 8: "I gave them the words you gave me"
>
> Verse 9 (see also v. 20): "I pray for them"
>
> Verse 12: "I protected them"
>
> Verse 18: "I have sent them into the world"
>
> Verse 19: "For them I sanctify myself"
>
> Verse 22: "I have given them the glory that you gave me"

These are seven things Jesus very clearly said He did in terms of making His disciples.

These are seven things Jesus very clearly said He did in terms of making His disciples. We want to study each of these and look at Jesus' life for how we can be more intentional about doing what Jesus did (John 14:12). John 17 will be our launching pad to study how Jesus made disciples.

But in order to appreciate John 17, we must understand the context around John 17.

In John 13, it is just a few hours before Jesus will be betrayed in the garden of Gethsemane. He takes His disciples on Thursday to a prepared upper room where they will celebrate His last Passover with them. He washes His disciples' feet and Judas leaves, setting up the betrayal. In John 14, Jesus gives some further instructions, telling them that He will be leaving them, and that they are to "do the works I have been doing, and they will do even greater things than these" (John 14:12).

At the end of John 14, Jesus says, "Come now; let us leave" (14:31). Jesus and His disciples left the upper room at this time.

Walking down toward the Water Gate and exiting the city walls, somewhere along the way Jesus stops and gives His teaching on the Vine and the branches (John 15:1–8). These are some of the last words Jesus says to His disciples, as He describes to them what they will face in their life. He continues this teaching into John 16.

Coming near the bottom of the Kidron Valley outside of the city walls, before Jesus crosses the Kidron Valley (see John 18:1–2), He stops and looks toward heaven and prays for His disciples.

I can see Jesus gathering His disciples around Himself, putting His hands upon them, and then passionately praying for them. We will study this prayer much more in the next few weeks.

But before we get to John 17, let's get to know the context.

Read this chapter below (John 13) and underline all the words that you see that emphasize the relational nature of Jesus' ministry. In the side bars, write why you consider Jesus' actions relational.

JOHN 13: JESUS WASHES HIS DISCIPLES' FEET

It was just before the Passover Festival. Jesus knew that the hour had come for him to leave this world and go to the Father. Having loved his own who were in the world, he loved them to the end.

2 The evening meal was in progress, and the devil had already prompted Judas, the son of Simon Iscariot, to betray Jesus. 3 Jesus knew that the Father had put all things under his power, and that he had come from God and was returning to God; 4 so he got up from the meal, took off his outer clothing, and wrapped a towel around his waist. 5 After that, he poured water into a basin and began to wash his disciples' feet, drying them with the towel that was wrapped around him.

6 He came to Simon Peter, who said to him, "Lord, are you going to wash my feet?" 7 Jesus replied, "You do not realize now what I am doing, but later you will under-stand."

8 "No," said Peter, "you shall never wash my feet."

Jesus answered, "Unless I wash you, you have no part with me."

⁹ "Then, Lord," Simon Peter replied, "not just my feet but my hands and my head as well!"

¹⁰ Jesus answered, "Those who have had a bath need only to wash their feet; their whole body is clean. And you are clean, though not every one of you." ¹¹ For he knew who was going to betray him, and that was why he said not every one was clean.

¹² When he had finished washing their feet, he put on his clothes and returned to his place. "Do you understand what I have done for you?" he asked them. ¹³ "You call me 'Teacher' and 'Lord,' and rightly so, for that is what I am. ¹⁴ Now that I, your Lord and Teacher, have washed your feet, you also should wash one another's feet. ¹⁵ I have set you an example that you should do as I have done for you. ¹⁶ Very truly I tell you, no servant is greater than his master, nor is a messenger greater than the one who sent him. ¹⁷ Now that you know these things, you will be blessed if you do them.

JESUS PREDICTS HIS BETRAYAL

¹⁸ "I am not referring to all of you; I know those I have chosen. But this is to fulfill this passage of Scripture: 'He who shared my bread has turned against me.'

¹⁹ "I am telling you now before it happens, so that when it does happen you will believe that I am who I am. ²⁰ Very truly I tell you, whoever accepts anyone I send accepts me; and whoever accepts me accepts the one who sent me."

²¹ After he had said this, Jesus was troubled in spirit and testified, "Very truly I tell you, one of you is going to betray me."

²² His disciples stared at one another, at a loss to know which of them he meant. ²³ One of them, the disciple whom Jesus loved, was reclining next to him. ²⁴ Simon Peter motioned to this disciple and said, "Ask him which one he means."

²⁵ Leaning back against Jesus, he asked him, "Lord, who is it?"

²⁶ Jesus answered, "It is the one to whom I will give this piece of bread when I have dipped it in the dish." Then, dipping the piece of bread, he gave it to Judas, the son of Simon Iscariot. ²⁷ As soon as Judas took the bread, Satan entered into him.

So Jesus told him, "What you are about to do, do quickly." ²⁸ But no one at the meal understood why Jesus said this to him. [29] Since Judas had charge of the money, some thought Jesus was telling him to buy what was needed for the festival, or to give something to the poor. [30] As soon as Judas had taken the bread, he went out. And it was night.

JESUS PREDICTS PETER'S DENIAL

[31] When he was gone, Jesus said, "Now the Son of Man is glorified and God is glorified in him. [32] If God is glorified in him, God will glorify the Son in himself, and will glorify him at once.

[33] "My children, I will be with you only a little longer. You will look for me, and just as I told the Jews, so I tell you now: Where I am going, you cannot come.

[34] "A new command I give you: Love one another. As I have loved you, so you must love one another. [35] By this everyone will know that you are my disciples, if you love one another."

[36] Simon Peter asked him, "Lord, where are you going?"

Jesus replied, "Where I am going, you cannot follow now, but you will follow later."

[37] Peter asked, "Lord, why can't I follow you now? I will lay down my life for you."

[38] Then Jesus answered, "Will you really lay down your life for me? Very truly I tell you, before the rooster crows, you will disown me three times!

Of all the words you have underlined, identify what you feel are the three key words that show Jesus was engaged in relational disciple-making. Explain why you chose these words.

God became flesh and made His dwelling among us (John 1:14). Jesus chose to impact people by "imparting His life" to them, a method that the apostle Paul spoke about in 1 Thessalonians 2:8. We can never forget that discipling is primarily relational. It is not just a curriculum we study or content that we learn (even though this is an important first step). It is far more, since we primarily learn through watching the lives of people we admire. Disciple-making begins and ends with healthy relationships, as modeled in Jesus' life with His disciples.

DAY TWO

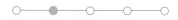

JOHN 14 AND RELATIONAL MINISTRY

Relational disciple-making happens when we use our life to invest in people, helping them to become more like Jesus. We all have a multitude of relationships, but some are more intensive than others.

Read John 14 below and identify the various kinds of relationships Jesus had in this chapter (i.e., the Twelve as a group, Thomas, Philip, His Father, the world, etc.). Be specific. List them below:

JOHN 14: JESUS COMFORTS HIS DISCIPLES

"Do not let your hearts be troubled. You believe in God; believe also in me. ² My Father's house has many rooms; if that were not so, would I have told you that I am going there to prepare a place for you? ³ And if I go and prepare a place for you, I will come back and take you to be with me that you also may be where I am. ⁴ You know the way to the place where I am going."

JESUS THE WAY TO THE FATHER

⁵ Thomas said to him, "Lord, we don't know where you are going, so how can we know the way?"

⁶ Jesus answered, "I am the way and the truth and the life. No one comes to the Father except through me. ⁷ If you really know me, you will know my Father as well. From now on, you do know him and have seen him."

⁸ Philip said, "Lord, show us the Father and that will be enough for us."

⁹ Jesus answered: "Don't you know me, Philip, even after I have been among you

such a long time? Anyone who has seen me has seen the Father. How can you say, 'Show us the Father'? [10] Don't you believe that I am in the Father, and that the Father is in me? The words I say to you I do not speak on my own authority. Rather, it is the Father, living in me, who is doing his work. [11] Believe me when I say that I am in the Father and the Father is in me; or at least believe on the evidence of the works themselves. [12] Very truly I tell you, whoever believes in me will do the works I have been doing, and they will do even greater things than these, because I am going to the Father. [13] And I will do whatever you ask in my name, so that the Father may be glorified in the Son. [14] You may ask me for anything in my name, and I will do it.

JESUS PROMISES THE HOLY SPIRIT

[15] "If you love me, keep my commands. [16] And I will ask the Father, and he will give you another advocate to help you and be with you forever— [17] the Spirit of truth. The world cannot accept him, because it neither sees him nor knows him. But you know him, for he lives with you and will be in you. [18] I will not leave you as orphans; I will come to you. [19] Before long, the world will not see me anymore, but you will see me. Because I live, you also will live. [20] On that day you will realize that I am in my Father, and you are in me, and I am in you. [21] Whoever has my commands and keeps them is the one who loves me. The one who loves me will be loved by my Father, and I too will love them and show myself to them."

[22] Then Judas (not Judas Iscariot) said, "But, Lord, why do you intend to show yourself to us and not to the world?"

[23] Jesus replied, "Anyone who loves me will obey my teaching. My Father will love them, and we will come to them and make our home with them. [24] Anyone who does not love me will not obey my teaching. These words you hear are not my own; they belong to the Father who sent me.

[25] "All this I have spoken while still with you. [26] But the Advocate, the Holy Spirit, whom the Father will send in my name, will teach you all things and will remind you of everything I have said to you. [27] Peace I leave with you; my peace I give you. I do not give to you as the world gives. Do not let your hearts be troubled and do not be afraid.

[28] "You heard me say, 'I am going away and I am coming back to you.' If you loved me, you would be glad that I am going to the Father, for the Father is greater than I. [29] I have told you now before it happens, so that when it does happen you will believe. [30] I will not say much more to you, for the prince of this world is coming. He has no hold over me, [31] but he comes so that the world may learn that I love the Father and do exactly what my Father has commanded me.

"Come now; let us leave.

Jesus had different kinds of relationships with different people. Those different kinds of relationships Jesus had required different types of responses. Identify how each relationship produced a different response from Jesus.

Person or relationship   **Jesus' response**

_____   _____

_____   _____

_____   _____

_____   _____

JOHN 15 AND RELATIONAL FRUITFULNESS

Relationships are often messy. When we become relationally engaged with people, we begin to see all their weaknesses as well as their strengths. Relationships can become demanding. They require time and energy.

Some people just seem to have an easier time with relationships than others. Some relationships just seem so sweet and natural—and at times, some relationships are just the opposite. Have you ever found yourself thinking, "Lord, I love You, but I just can't stand people"? If we ever start thinking like this, what does 1 John 4:19–21 remind us about?

John 15 uses many words to describe the type of relationship the Lord wants with and from us. Read John 15:1–17 below. Identify some of the words Jesus uses to define that type of relationship.

Clarify what you feel is the single most critical lesson to learn about our relationship with God. (See especially verses 1–17.)

John 15:18–27 clarifies our relationship with the world. Again, many relational words are used to describe that relationship with the world. Read verses 18–27 and write out those words that define that relationship.

What would you identify as the single most critical lesson to learn about our relationship with the world? (See especially verses 18–27.)

JOHN 15: THE VINE AND THE BRANCHES

"I am the true vine, and my Father is the gardener. [2] He cuts off every branch in me that bears no fruit, while every branch that does bear fruit he prunes so that it will be even more fruitful. [3] You are already clean because of the word I have spoken to you. [4] Remain in me, as I also remain in you. No branch can bear fruit by itself; it must remain in the vine. Neither can you bear fruit unless you remain in me.

[5] "I am the vine; you are the branches. If you remain in me and I in you, you will bear much fruit; apart from me you can do nothing. [6] If you do not remain in me, you are like a branch that is thrown away and withers; such branches are picked up, thrown into the fire and burned. [7] If you remain in me and my words remain in you, ask whatever you wish, and it will be done for you. [8] This is to my Father's glory, that you bear much fruit, showing yourselves to be my disciples.

[9] "As the Father has loved me, so have I loved you. Now remain in my love. [10] If you keep my commands, you will remain in my love, just as I have kept my Father's commands and remain in his love. [11] I have told you this so that my joy may be in you and that your joy may be complete. [12] My command is this: Love each other as I have loved you. [13] Greater love has no one than this: to lay down one's life for

one's friends. [14] You are my friends if you do what I command. [15] I no longer call you servants, because a servant does not know his master's business. Instead, I have called you friends, for everything that I learned from my Father I have made known to you. [16] You did not choose me, but I chose you and appointed you so that you might go and bear fruit—fruit that will last—and so that whatever you ask in my name the Father will give you. [17] This is my command: Love each other.

THE WORLD HATES THE DISCIPLES

[18] "If the world hates you, keep in mind that it hated me first. [19] If you belonged to the world, it would love you as its own. As it is, you do not belong to the world, but I have chosen you out of the world. That is why the world hates you. [20] Remember what I told you: 'A servant is not greater than his master.' If they persecuted me, they will persecute you also. If they obeyed my teaching, they will obey yours also. [21] They will treat you this way because of my name, for they do not know the one who sent me. [22] If I had not come and spoken to them, they would not be guilty of sin; but now they have no excuse for their sin. [23] Whoever hates me hates my Father as well. [24] If I had not done among them the works no one else did, they would not be guilty of sin. As it is, they have seen, and yet they have hated both me and my Father. [25] But this is to fulfill what is written in their Law: 'They hated me without reason.'

THE WORK OF THE HOLY SPIRIT

[26] "When the Advocate comes, whom I will send to you from the Father—the Spirit of truth who goes out from the Father—he will testify about me. [27] And you also must testify, for you have been with me from the beginning.

Relationships were not a strategy for Jesus. They were a way of life. Therefore we must remember that any disciple-making that is void of an ongoing relational emphasis lacks the impact of Jesus' method. To Jesus, relational disciple-making was a nonnegotiable.

DAY FOUR

JOHN 16 AND RELATIONAL DISCIPLE-MAKING

Relational disciple-making is hard for several reasons. First, it is hard because to genuinely love someone and invest in them demands time and energy. In our limited humanity, we can only genuinely invest in a small number of people. While we may have many acquaintances, we only have time to invest in a few disciples. Jesus understood this. He ministered at times to the crowds, but he intentionally poured into a few—twelve, to be exact. This is the "genius of Christ's strategy."[1]

Secondly, relational disciple-making is hard because as we begin to genuinely love our disciples and invest in them, we also begin to truly carry a new level of concern and burden for them.

Read John 16 below, and describe (or underline) some of the concerns that Jesus had for His disciples:

JOHN 16

"All this I have told you so that you will not fall away. [2] They will put you out of the synagogue; in fact, the time is coming when anyone who kills you will think they are offering a service to God. [3] They will do such things because they have not known the Father or me. [4] I have told you this, so that when their time comes you will remember that I warned you about them. I did not tell you this from the beginning because I was with you, [5] but now I am going to him who sent me. None of you asks me, 'Where are you going?' [6] Rather, you are filled with grief because I have said these things. [7] But very truly I tell you, it is for your good that I am going away. Unless I go away, the Advocate will not come to you; but if I go, I will send him to you. [8] When he comes, he will prove the world to be in the wrong about sin and righteousness and judgment: [9] about sin, because people do not believe in me; [10] about righteousness, because I am going to the Father, where you can see me no longer; [11] and about judgment, because the prince of this world now stands condemned.

[12] "I have much more to say to you, more than you can now bear. [13] But when he, the Spirit of truth, comes, he will guide you into all the truth. He will not speak on his own; he will speak only what he hears, and he will tell you what is yet to come. [14] He will glorify me because it is from me that he will receive what he will make known to you. [15] All that belongs to the Father is mine. That is why I said the Spirit will receive from me what he will make known to you."

THE DISCIPLES' GRIEF WILL TURN TO JOY

[16] Jesus went on to say, "In a little while you will see me no more, and then after a little while you will see me."

[17] At this, some of his disciples said to one another, "What does he mean by say-ing, 'In a little while you will see me no more, and then after a little while you will see me,' and 'Because I am going to the Father'?" [18] They kept asking, "What does he mean by 'a little while'? We don't understand what he is saying."

[19] Jesus saw that they wanted to ask him about this, so he said to them, "Are you asking one another what I meant when I said, 'In a little while you will see me no more, and then after a little while you will see me'? [20] Very truly I tell you, you will weep and mourn while the world rejoices. You will grieve, but your grief will turn to joy. [21] A woman giving birth to a child has pain because her time has come; but when her baby is born she forgets the anguish because of her joy that a child is born into the world. [22] So with you: Now is your time of grief, but I will see you again and you will rejoice, and no one will take away your joy. [23] In that day you will no longer ask me anything. Very truly I tell you, my Father will give you whatever you ask in my name. [24] Until now you have not asked for anything in my name. Ask and you will receive, and your joy will be complete.

[25] "Though I have been speaking figuratively, a time is coming when I will no longer use this kind of language but will tell you plainly about my Father. [26] In that day you will ask in my name. I am not saying that I will ask the Father on your behalf. [27] No, the Father himself loves you because you have loved me and have believed that I

came from God. [28] I came from the Father and entered the world; now I am leaving the world and going back to the Father."

[29] Then Jesus' disciples said, "Now you are speaking clearly and without figures of speech. [30] Now we can see that you know all things and that you do not even need to have anyone ask you questions. This makes us believe that you came from God."

[31] "Do you now believe?" Jesus replied. [32] "A time is coming and in fact has come when you will be scattered, each to your own home. You will leave me all alone. Yet I am not alone, for my Father is with me.

[33] "I have told you these things, so that in me you may have peace. In this world you will have trouble. But take heart! I have overcome the world."

What can we learn about how Jesus handled all the concerns of His relational investment in people? In other words, what would Jesus' advice to us be if we find ourselves stressed out because of "concerns" we have for our disciples?

DAY FIVE

JOHN 17 AND JESUS' OWN PRIORITIES

John 17 is made up of the longest prayer recorded in the New Testament and definitely the longest prayer recorded by Jesus. In it we have a chance to listen in on the Father and Son's intimate communication with each other.

As Jesus comes near the Kidron Valley, just before He crosses over into the garden of Gethsemane (John 18:1–2), I can visualize Jesus gathering His loved disciples around Him, kneeling with them in a huddle, and then looking toward heaven, praying this prayer. It obviously impacted the disciples, as John, through the Holy Spirit, recalled years later what He prayed.

Earlier in this week's study, I stated that John 17 identifies seven disciplines (priorities) of how Jesus made disciples. Read through John 17 and see if you can identify the seven things Jesus said He did as He discipled His disciples (don't peek at the answer in the introduction!). Some are repeated twice. Look for seven things that Jesus said He did for His disciples:

John 17 identifies seven disciplines (priorities) of how Jesus made disciples.

1. _____

2. _____

3. _____

4. _____

5. _____

6. _____

7. _____

JOHN 17: JESUS PRAYS TO BE GLORIFIED

After Jesus said this, he looked toward heaven and prayed:

"Father, the hour has come. Glorify your Son, that your Son may glorify you. ² For you granted him authority over all people that he might give eternal life to all those you have given him. ³ Now this is eternal life: that they know you, the only true God, and Jesus Christ, whom you have sent. ⁴ I have brought you glory on earth by finishing the work you gave me to do. ⁵ And now, Father, glorify me in your presence with the glory I had with you before the world began.

JESUS PRAYS FOR HIS DISCIPLES

⁶ "I have revealed you to those whom you gave me out of the world. They were yours; you gave them to me and they have obeyed your word. ⁷ Now they know that everything you have given me comes from you. ⁸ For I gave them the words you gave me and they accepted them. They knew with certainty that I came from you, and they believed that you sent me. ⁹ I pray for them. I am not praying for the world, but for those you have given me, for they are yours. ¹⁰ All I have is yours, and all you have is mine. And glory has come to me through them. ¹¹ I will remain in the world no longer, but they are still in the world, and I am coming to you. Holy Father, protect them by the power of your name, the name you gave me, so that they may be one as we are one. ¹² While I was with them, I protected them and kept them safe by that name you gave me. None has been lost except the one doomed to destruction so that Scripture would be fulfilled.

¹³ "I am coming to you now, but I say these things while I am still in the world, so that they may have the full measure of my joy within them. ¹⁴ I have given them your word and the world has hated them, for they are not of the world any more than I am of the world. ¹⁵ My prayer is not that you take them out of the world but that you protect them from the evil one. ¹⁶ They are not of the world, even as I am not of it. ¹⁷ Sanctify them by the truth; your word is truth. ¹⁸ As you sent me into the world, I have sent them into the world. ¹⁹ For them I sanctify myself, that they too may be truly sanctified.

JESUS PRAYS FOR ALL BELIEVERS

²⁰ "My prayer is not for them alone. I pray also for those who will believe in me through their message, ²¹ that all of them may be one, Father, just as you are in

me and I am in you. May they also be in us so that the world may believe that you have sent me. [22] I have given them the glory that you gave me, that they may be one as we are one—[23] I in them and you in me—so that they may be brought to complete unity. Then the world will know that you sent me and have loved them even as you have loved me.

[24] "Father, I want those you have given me to be with me where I am, and to see my glory, the glory you have given me because you loved me before the creation of the world.

[25] "Righteous Father, though the world does not know you, I know you, and they know that you have sent me. [26] I have made you known to them, and will continue to make you known in order that the love you have for me may be in them and that I myself may be in them."

Which of these seven "I" statements do you most clearly associate with? Which one means the most to you?

Which of these seven "I" statements do you least understand? That is, identify any "I" statement for which the meaning is unclear to you.

TAKING THE NEXT STEP:

Before we finish this week's study, take a few minutes to identify the people the Lord has put into your life that you need to develop deeper relationships with. Of all your relationships, whom do you think the Lord wants you to invest in (disciple) on a deeper level?

List them on the next page and then identify what stage in their disciple-making journey they are in—a seeker, a new believer, a growing worker, a mature disciple-maker? (These four categories are developed in my book *4 Chair Discipling*, which describes them as Chair 1, 2, 3, and 4 people.) You can write your names in the Circle of Concern cards in the back and place it in your Bible as a reminder to pray.

Name	Stage of Disciple-making	Next Steps I Can Take
1. _____	_____	_____
		_____
		_____
		_____
2. _____	_____	_____
		_____
		_____
		_____
3. _____	_____	_____
		_____
		_____
		_____
4. _____	_____	_____
		_____
		_____
		_____
5. _____	_____	_____
		_____
		_____
		_____
6. _____	_____	_____
		_____
		_____
		_____

INTENTIONAL: "I WILL MAKE YOU"

(MATTHEW 4:19B ESV)

Go deeper: Watch videos online and download the Like Jesus app. LikeJesus.church/live

GETTING STARTED

When I was a young Christian and a new youth pastor, a professor at Bible school challenged me to study the life of Christ chronologically. He encouraged me to get a harmony of the Gospels and study how Jesus made disciples, in chronological order. (A harmony of the Gospels takes the four Gospels and seeks to lay out their stories, side by side, in chronological order.) I took my professor's challenge and, using a harmony, I began to analyze what Christ did the first year of His ministry, the second year, the third year, and the last year.

One of the first conclusions I came to in studying Jesus this way was how intentional He was in making disciples who could make other disciples.

In my most recent book, *4 Chair Discipling*, I analyzed that intentionality by looking at four challenges Jesus gave to His disciples as they grew and matured in what He called them to do. But for those of you not familiar with that book, let me give you a quick overview of the process.

Right after being baptized by His cousin John, Jesus is led by the Spirit into the wilderness. Immediately after coming out of the wilderness, Jesus goes back to where John was baptizing. John points to Jesus and says, "Look, the Lamb of God, who takes away the sin of the world!" (John 1:29). Testifying that he would not have known who the

Messiah was, except that he saw the "Spirit come down and remain" on Him, John points to Jesus as the Messiah (John 1:33). Two of John's disciples, Andrew and, we assume, John, immediately move toward Jesus (John 1:37).

Jesus gives His first challenge to them: "Come and you will see" (John 1:39 ESV). This is a low-level challenge, simply meaning "just show up." These two disciples go to where Jesus is staying and have at least a two-hour conversation with Him.[1] Andrew runs out to find his brother Peter, telling him, "We have found the Messiah" (John 1:41). Jesus obviously sensed their seeker hearts, opened the Scriptures to them and showed them why He was the promised Messiah, and then challenged them to follow Him.

The second challenge comes soon on the heels of this challenge and is given to Philip. Philip could have been traveling and staying with his hometown friends Andrew and Peter. Jesus, after deciding to head back to Galilee, found Philip and said to him, "Follow me" (John 1:43)—a very different challenge in the Greek (*akoulatheow*). It literally means to walk behind, follow in my steps, and learn of me. It was a challenge often given to disciples from a Rabbi teacher.

Eighteen months later, after spending considerable time with these new seekers and followers, Jesus moves from Nazareth to Capernaum. John has been put in prison and so now Jesus picks up the message of John (Matt. 4:17) and approaches what I like to call His "starting five" (James, John, Simon, Andrew, and later Matthew). He puts all these challenges together with a deeper third challenge, "Follow me," Jesus said, "and I will make you fishers of men" (Matt. 4:19 ESV). In this phrase where Jesus says, "I will make you," it literally means that He would show them how, to prepare them to do, to produce (*poieo* in the Greek) this in their lives. It is a word with intentionality and we will study how Jesus did this.

Lastly, toward the end of His time with the disciples, in John 15:16 Jesus challenges them to now "go and bear fruit." "You did not choose me, but I chose you and appointed you . . . whatever you ask in my name the Father will give you" (John 15:16). This word "go" literally means "go away, leave, or depart." This challenge was to now do what they had been equipped to do—bear fruit in His name.

As I have studied the life of Christ over the last thirty-five years, I have been amazed at how Jesus so masterfully developed His disciples by challenging them to different

While fully listening to His Father's leadership through the Holy Spirit, Jesus intentionally developed His disciples to become disciple-makers—disciples who disciple others.

levels of involvement with Him. Taking "unschooled, ordinary men" (Acts 4:13), Jesus trained them, sent them out, and empowered them to "turn[] the world upside down" (Acts 17:6 ESV).

While fully listening to His Father's leadership through the Holy Spirit, Jesus intentionally developed His disciples to become disciple-makers—disciples who disciple others. Upon seeing His disciples being used to share the good news with others, right toward the very end of His ministry we are told that Jesus was "full of joy through the Holy Spirit" (Luke 10:21). Jesus now knew that His work was done (John 17:4) and He could go to the cross, accomplishing the will of the Father, and atone for the sins of the world. Leaving behind the gift of eternal life (John 17:3) by destroying the works of Satan (Heb. 2:14), Jesus could rest in knowing that His disciples could go and reproduce in others what had been produced in them. The Bible calls this "fruit."

During this week's study, my prayer is that you too will see the intentionality of Jesus in developing His disciples. Remember, our calling is to "walk as Jesus did" (1 John 2:6 NIV1984), doing what Jesus did (John 14:12).

Before you begin this week's study, what are some ways that you think Jesus was very intentional in what He did? Try to list at least three ways, giving specific Scriptures to back them up (if you can).

Intentionality   Scripture

1. _____   _____

2. _____   _____

3. _____   _____

JESUS' FIRST MISSION TRIP

Jesus was so intentional that He took His disciples on at least five mission trips and seven fishing trips. All of these were intended to train them to become "fishers of men."

While it's important not to oversimplify the life of Christ or misstate what He did, let me try to explain my understanding. A "mission trip" is a longer venture by which Jesus takes His disciples out of their comfort zone and sometimes into cross-cultural experiences. A "fishing trip" is an intentional experience through which Jesus is modeling or training His disciples in creative ways to share the good news of the kingdom. Every day this week, we will look at five mission trips and seven fishing trips.

Early in the ministry of Jesus (approximately the first 15–18 months), Jesus tells us that He "had to go through Samaria" (John 4:4). For some of you, this is a very familiar story. But for others of you, this is a brand-new story. I'd like you to reread the story in John 4 in your Bible, and ask yourselves these questions:

What do you think are the primary lessons Jesus wants His disciples to learn from this experience? Try to identify what you think are the top three lessons:

What new insights do you think the disciples were experiencing as they went through Samaria?

What new insights did they gain as they saw Jesus talking to the woman?

What about when they saw the whole town coming out to Jesus—any new insights here?

What about when they sat under Jesus' instructions (vv. 34–38)?

Any new insights as they watched the response of the town after two days of being with them?

This trip truly impacted Jesus' early disciples. They saw Him travel to a place most good Jews would never step foot in. They saw Him talking with a woman—something no Jewish man would ever do in public. They heard Him say that "the harvest was ripe," only to open their eyes and see the whole town coming out to learn more. And, they watched Jesus for two days interact with the Samaritans, many of whom became believers. What a remarkable trip for these new disciples of Jesus!

DAY TWO

FISHING TRIPS #1–3

Working chronologically (a harmony of the Gospels shows us this), we now find Jesus in Galilee. As you put Matthew 4:12–22 with Mark 1:14–20 chronologically, you see several events unfold.

We are eighteen months into the ministry of Christ, and John the Baptist has been put in prison (Mark 1:14; Matt. 4:12). Jesus makes the decision to move from His hometown of Nazareth and set up His ministry headquarters in the more populated region of Capernaum by the Sea of Galilee. All of this was to fulfill the prophecy of Isaiah 9:1–2, "in the past he humbled the land of Zebulun and the land of Naphtali, but in the future he will honor Galilee of the nations, by the Way of the Sea, beyond the Jordan—The people walking in darkness have seen a great light; on those living in the land of deep darkness a light has dawned." Nazareth was on the edge of Zebulun and Capernaum was in Naphtali, fulfilling this exact prophecy.

As the crowds begin to grow, Jesus knows He must go deeper with a few. He now approaches His "starting five" (not yet the Twelve) and challenges them to come closer—"Follow me, and I will make you fishers of men" (Matt. 4:19 ESV).

Immediately, Jesus takes His disciples on His first three fishing trips to help them become "fishers of men." Let's see what we can learn from Jesus.

FISHING TRIP #1

Read Mark 1:21–28. What do you think Jesus wanted to model to His disciples in this experience?

Among what type of people did Jesus conduct this outreach event or experience?

Imagine you are one of Jesus' starting five and all of this is new to you. In what ways do you think you would most be impacted by this experience? Explain.

What do you think was the disciples' role in this ministry experience? Do you think they did anything during or after this event (look closely)? Explain your conclusions.

FISHING TRIP #2

Read Mark 1:29–31. Where was this fishing trip conducted, and with whom?

How do you think a sick mother-in-law would impact Peter's family life?

What do you think Jesus wanted His disciples to learn in this ministry experience?

Creatively (in the Spirit) try to describe what Peter's home was like after this event.

What involvement, if any, do you think the disciples had in this ministry experience?

FISHING TRIP #3

Read Mark 1:32–37. Where was this fishing trip conducted? Who was involved?

In what ways, if any, do you think the disciples of Jesus were involved in this ministry outreach?

What was Jesus modeling in this event?

What do you think Jesus' disciples learned from this event that was different from the other events?

What happened after this event (early the next morning)? What was Jesus modeling here, and what do you think the disciples learned?

TAKING THE NEXT STEP:

Has anyone ever intentionally helped you share your faith or modeled in front of you how to do that? What could you do to put yourself in a position to learn from someone in this area?

Who do you know that does this well? What characteristics do you think make them successful at sharing their faith?

DAY THREE

MISSION TRIP #2 AND FISHING TRIP #4

MISSION TRIP #2

Jesus now takes His disciples out on a lengthier trip. Josephus, a first-century Jewish historian, says there were 204 villages in Galilee that were large enough to have synagogues. We don't know how many of these Jesus visited on this mission trip, but it was probably a lengthy time for His disciples to be away from family and friends. (The length of this trip will play into the next fishing trip we look at in Luke 5:1–11.)

Read Mark 1:38–39. To whom was Jesus now ministering as He and His disciples traveled together?

Jesus was repeating what He did in Mark 1:21–26. There is often great value in repetition, especially if we are seeking to train someone. Think of something that others think is hard, but you feel comfortable doing. Write it below and explain why it feels easy for you.

How do you think the disciples may have become increasingly involved as they traveled with Jesus to all the synagogues? Understanding that the average synagogue was quite small, and assuming that Jesus was intentionally using this experience to develop His disciples' skills, use your sanctified imagination and try to think of skills Jesus intentionally developed in His disciples. List them below and explain how these skills could have been valuable later, after Jesus ascended into heaven:

FISHING TRIP #4

Read Luke 5:1–11. Luke inserts an interesting event in his gospel. After returning from preaching in the synagogues, we are told that the disciples return to their fishing. Why would that be necessary for the disciples, especially Peter?

Fishing by nets, on the shores of Galilee, is often done in the shallow waters of the north shore when the fish come up in the coolness of the evening. Upon returning with Jesus from the preaching tour in the synagogues, I'm sure the disciples needed to get back to work for simple financial reasons. They needed to pay bills and restore their loss of income during their exciting mission trip with Jesus.

How had this night of fishing gone for the disciples? What kind of mood do you think they were in?

I like to think that Peter's wife (let's call her Ruthie) was happy that Peter was hanging out with Jesus (who had healed her mom). But she may also have been concerned about paying the bills. If this was true about Ruthie, how might Luke 5:5 take on a new meaning?

With the possible concern from the family to pay bills, why would Luke 5:6–10 take on a whole new meaning?

In just a few minutes, Peter caught so many fish that the boats began to sink. Have you ever experienced God providing for you in a miraculous way when you had given of your time and resources to serve Him? Describe it below:

Why is this lesson about God's faithful provision so critical to anyone who wants to follow Jesus wholeheartedly, like Peter in Luke 5:10–11?

TAKING THE NEXT STEP:

Stop right now and thank the Lord specifically for the times He has provided for you.

DAY FOUR

MISSION TRIPS #3-5

MISSION TRIP #3

It is not totally possible to identify dates for each event in the Gospels, but the mission trips seem to be about six months apart. The first was eighteen months into the ministry of Christ. The second was about two years into Christ's ministry. Now the next three are about six months apart, with the last one being right at the end of His three and three-quarter year ministry. As I look at this, I can't help but feel how intentional Jesus was as He developed His disciples. Each trip becomes harder. Each trip engages the disciples on a deeper level.

Let's now look at the next three mission trips.

Read Luke 8:1–4. This is at least two and a half years into Christ's ministry, after He has expanded beyond His "starting five." Who else was traveling with Jesus now?

Where were they now traveling, and what size crowds were they encountering?

What do you think were some of the unique lessons the disciples were learning in these trips that they might not have learned from His work in the synagogues?

I can't help but feel how intentional Jesus was as He developed His disciples. Each trip becomes harder. Each trip engages the disciples on a deeper level.

What do you know about Mary Magdalene or Joanna? We now have a presence of women disciples with Jesus. How might their presence change the lessons the disciples learn—especially for the male disciples?

MISSION TRIP #4

Read Matthew 9:35–10:5 and Luke 9:1–2. This experience is about three years into Jesus' ministry. How do you see the disciples' involvement now increasing?

What unique lessons do you think the disciples were now learning?

MISSION TRIP #5

Read Luke 10:1–21. We are now about three and a half years into Jesus' ministry. He is making His way to Jerusalem for His final Passover. Jesus now sends out seventy-two disciples. Six months earlier, Jesus sent out the Twelve, two by two. Now He has seventy-two going out two by two. While I can't substantiate this, it is interesting to consider that maybe each of the six teams of two from the original Twelve had now developed their own groups of disciples and were learning to oversee six more teams of twelve (6 x 12 = 72). Could it be possible that Jesus was beginning to encourage and model multiplication?

What unique lessons were the disciples learning in this mission trip? (See vv. 5–9, 16–17, 18–21.)

What was Jesus' response in Luke 10:21? Why do you think we have this response recorded from Jesus? What about this could cause Jesus to respond this way?

DAY FIVE

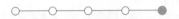

FISHING TRIPS #5–7

FISHING TRIP #5

I've always found it interesting how Jesus takes the known to help us move into the unknown. Here, Jesus takes fishermen and challenges them to become "fishers of men."

Read Mark 1:40–45.

What unique things were the disciples learning from this "fishing for men" experience?

How would this event impact the disciples' worldview? What type of person, in the minds of the disciples, was this outreach to?

FISHING TRIP #6

Read Mark 2:1–12. What was unique about this "fishing for men" trip?

What specifically did Jesus want His disciples to learn from this event? (See v. 10.)

As the disciples were watching all of this happen, what other lessons do you think they were observing?

The very fact that Christ became flesh and dwelt among us proves how He engaged relationally in His disciples' lives.

FISHING TRIP #7

Read Mark 2:13–17. Tax collectors were considered traitors by Jews, since they were helping the oppressive enemy. They were often hated by the Jewish people, since they could line their own pockets with the extra taxes they collected. Think about who Matthew was and who his friends were. Look carefully at what Jesus says in verses 15–17. What unique lessons do you think Jesus wants His disciples to learn from this situation?

TAKING THE NEXT STEP:

What are some events or experiences that are offered in your community or church that would put you in a position to allow the Lord to make you more of a fisher of men? Remember, it is the Lord who said He'd intentionally help you in this area ("I will make you . . ." [ESV])!

What are some things you could do with your disciples to help them become more like Jesus in this area? Don't make this complicated. Jesus wants us to use the everyday events of life.

After studying these mission trips and fishing trips, would you agree that Jesus was intentional in developing His disciples?

Yes_____ No_____ Sort of_____ Explain your answer:

_____

_____

_____

_____

_____

So far in this study we have been discussing what it means to make disciples the way Jesus did. First, we observed how Jesus was engaged relationally in His disciples' lives. The very fact that He became flesh and dwelt among us should prove this point. But beyond that we find Jesus investing heavily in a few disciples, teaching them to do the same. Second, we observed how intentional Jesus was in teaching His disciples how to multiply into others. We looked in this chapter at Jesus' mission and fishing trips.

In the next seven chapters we will look at seven very practical things Jesus Himself said He did as He intentionally poured into His disciples. We will seek to discern practical lessons for disciple-making from Jesus' words and the model of His life.

7 DISCIPLINES OF A DISCIPLE-MAKER

PRACTICAL "METHODS" JESUS USED TO MAKE DISCIPLES

M any authors who write about John 17 find themselves overwhelmed with the impact of the chapter.

Philip Melanchthon who, along with Martin Luther was a towering intellect of the early Reformation, said, "There is no voice which has ever been heard, either in heaven or in earth, more exalted, more holy, more fruitful, more sublime, than the prayer offered up by the Son of God Himself."[1]

Merrill Tenney calls the prayer in John 17 the "farewell prayer of Jesus for His disciples,"[2] and clams that "in reading it, men are listening to the family conversation of deity."[3]

Kent Hughes records this in his commentary on John: "John 17 is one of the greatest chapters in the Bible, and certainly one of the most treasured. Some refer to it as the 'Holy of Holies of Sacred Scripture.'"[4]

Scholars and students of the Bible throughout the generations have regarded John 17 as one of the most amazing passages of Scripture.

Six times in these verses, Jesus states that His disciples are the Father's gift to Him (John 17:2, 6, 9, 24). So often we tend to think only in terms of Jesus being God's gift to us. But this prayer reveals that Jesus knew the disciples were the Father's "love gift" to Him. And it is because of this that He prays passionately for them as His final act before going into the garden to be betrayed.

There are so many ways this chapter could be studied, but for the purposes of this book, we will look primarily at what Jesus says in His own words—what He prioritized with these disciples. These actions are the "seven disciplines of a disciple-maker."

For the next seven weeks, we will spend a week looking at each of these actions individually. There are very specific "I" statements in John 17. They are:

John 17:6 (see also v. 26): "I have revealed you to those whom you gave me"
Verse 8—"I gave them the words You gave Me"
Verses 9 (see also v. 20)—"I pray for them"
Verse 12—"I protected them"
Verse 18—"I have sent them into the world"

So often we tend to think only in terms of Jesus being God's gift to us. But this prayer reveals that Jesus knew the disciples were the Father's "love gift" to Him.

Verse 19—"I sanctify myself"

Verse 22—"I have given them the glory that you gave me"

These statements, these seven actions of Jesus, can be simplified in seven words: Reveal, Speak, Pray, Protect, Send, Sanctify, and Share. Reveal the Father to your disciples; speak His words into their lives; pray regularly for them; protect them; send them out; sanctify yourself for their sake; and share the glory with them. These seven words are insight into how Jesus made His disciples. Let's now take a deeper look. To simplify even further, you might think of these words as one R (reveal), four Ss (speak, send, sanctify, share) and 2 Ps (pray and protect).

For the next few weeks, we will only have four days of study for each week. The reason for this is that we will use each day to look at what Jesus did with His disciples as they developed and matured through four challenges: come and see (seekers), follow me (new believers), follow me and fish for men (workers), and go and bear fruit (mature disciple-makers). In the following lessons, where possible, day 1 will focus on seekers, day 2 will focus on followers, day 3 will focus on the few workers, and day 4 will focus on mature disciplers.

—

REVEAL: "I HAVE REVEALED YOU TO THOSE WHOM YOU GAVE ME"

(JOHN 17:6)

Go deeper: Watch videos online and download the Like Jesus app. LikeJesus.church/live

GETTING STARTED

Try to imagine with me the emotions of the last few weeks of Jesus' ministry.

As Jesus "resolutely set out for Jerusalem" (Luke 9:51), He sent His workers ahead of Him two by two. They returned "with joy" and Jesus was "full of joy" by the Holy Spirit (Luke 10:21). As Jesus saw His disciples sharing the good news, He knew His three years of investing in them would now yield the intended fruit of multiplication.

Jesus made His way to Jericho and began His final ascent into Jerusalem. For the third time, He told His disciples that He must go to Jerusalem, suffer many things, be mocked and mistreated, spit upon, scourged, and ultimately killed (Luke 18:32–33). Mark tells us that those who followed Jesus were fearful because they knew that a confrontation lay ahead (Mark 10:32).

As they made their way to Jerusalem, an uphill journey of more than eighteen miles, the crowds in the temple were buzzing. "What do you think? Isn't he coming to the

> As Jesus saw His disciples sharing the good news, He knew His three years of investing in them would now yield the intended fruit of multiplication.

festival at all?" (John 11:56). The Pharisees had given orders that "anyone who found out where Jesus was should report it so that they might arrest him" (John 11:57).

Stopping in Bethany, Mary boldly anointed Jesus' feet. This caused a major controversy among the disciples (Matt. 26:6–13). As the multitudes heard that Jesus was in Bethany, many went out to Him, wanting to see Lazarus whom Jesus had raised from the dead. This caused the chief priests to plot to kill Lazarus also (John 12:10).

Making His move toward the Mount of Olives, Jesus mounted a colt. The multitudes were going in front of Him and many others followed. As the crowds approached the back side of the Mount of Olives, a great multitude that had come to the feast heard that Jesus was coming to Jerusalem. They took branches from the palm trees and went out to meet Him. As the two groups met, they cried out in a loud voice, "Hosanna! Blessed is he who comes in the name of the Lord! Blessed is the king of Israel" (John 12:12–13).

We are told the "whole city was stirred" (Matt. 21:10). As Jesus walked down the Mount of Olives, while the crowds were rejoicing, Jesus "wept" (Luke 19:41).

The week was filled with teaching, controversy, and conflict. On Monday, Jesus cleansed the temple for a second time (Luke 19:45–48) and cursed the fig tree (Mark 11:12–14). On Tuesday, He spent the day confronting the scribes and Pharisees, and "many even among the leaders believed in him" (John 12:42). After the Olivet Discourse (Matt. 24), Jesus predicted the sad destruction of the city. Wednesday is the silent day, probably when Judas made his move to betray Jesus. Thursday, Jesus has His disciples prepare for the Passover meal, and the historic events of the upper room (John 13–16) took place.

Imagine the emotions of the crowds during this week! The chatter, the discussion, the questions! Imagine the emotions of Jesus' mother Mary—what she must have pondered in her heart. Imagine the emotions of the disciples, who in the garden could not stay awake because they were "exhausted from sorrow" (Luke 22:45).

Imagine the emotions of Jesus. Three times in the last few weeks He wept—over Lazarus, over Jerusalem, and in the garden.

How does the fullness of this week, both in the disciples' lives and in Jesus' life, cause you to think about the emotion in Jesus' prayer in John 17? How would you describe the condition of His heart at this moment?

Read John 12:23–28. Does what Jesus says here change anything about what you answered above?

Now read John 17:1–5. What most stands out to you as you read this passage?

Jesus says in John 17:4, "I have brought you glory on earth by finishing the work you gave me to do." Some people believe Jesus is referring here to His death on the cross. But many others, myself included, have a different interpretation. Since Jesus hasn't died yet, it's likely that the "work" Jesus references in this passage is making disciples that He is now going to pray for. If Jesus brought glory to His Father by making disciples, what does this say about how we glorify the Father?

In 17:6, Jesus mentions the first action that He had done with His disciples. "I have revealed you to those whom you gave me." Based upon your knowledge of Christ, list any ways that Jesus is "revealing" the Father to His disciples. Be as specific as you can.

DAY ONE

REVEALED: SHOWING UP AND BEING PRESENT

The word "revealed" used in John 17:6 is the first of the phrases Jesus uses to describe His priorities with His disciples. The Greek word used here literally means to "openly manifest, to be present, to appear."

But before we go too far, read John 17:6–7 carefully. Write out these verses below, underlining what you think are some key words.

What can we learn from these verses about Jesus' disciples? List everything you see in John 17:6–7.

What do you think verse 7 is saying about how Jesus "revealed" the Father to them?

The incarnation of Jesus is perhaps the greatest miracle of all. God's Son adds humanity to His deity. He becomes like us as the forever God/Man, bridging the chasm between sinful man and the holiness of God.

God showed up in our world, became like us in every way, and lived in our midst. For thirty years, he lived in a small town, working in the marketplace. He lived among us and learned our language, experienced our joys and sorrows, and experienced every aspect of our lives, yet without sin.

Read John 1:14. What do you see are the major surprises about this incarnation?

The word "dwelling" literally means "tabernacle" or "make one's presence among." From God's perspective, how radical of a move was this? Explain why.

God showed up in our world, became like us in every way, and lived in our midst.

GRACE AND TRUTH

Read the last part of John 1:14. This verse describes how Jesus revealed His glory among us, "full of grace and truth." If Jesus had been gracious but not truthful, what would that have looked like?

If Jesus had been just truthful but not gracious, what would that have looked like?

Why were both grace and truth necessary to properly reveal the Father to His disciples?

GRACE AND TRUTH WITH SEEKERS

In John 3, Nicodemus comes to Jesus by night, seeking to know more. As you read John 3:1–17, list examples of "grace" and examples of "truth."

Grace   Truth

_____   _____
_____   _____
_____   _____
_____   _____
_____   _____
_____   _____

In Luke 4:16–30, where do you see both "grace" and "truth"?

Grace   Truth

_____   _____
_____   _____
_____   _____
_____   _____
_____   _____
_____   _____

What do you think Jesus' disciples were learning about the character of God as they watched Jesus with seekers (Nicodemus and in His hometown)? Why was this so valuable to the disciples?

Who are some of the seekers (nonbelievers) God has placed in your life (family members, neighbors, coworkers, friends, etc.)? List them below, and then you may want to place them in Your Circles on page 173.

As you think about these seekers, what does both "grace and truth" look like in your relationships with them? Which of the two are you better at? How can you improve in the other?

Jesus revealed Himself to His disciples. He did this with both grace and truth. By doing so, He perfectly showed us the character of God and how God desires us to interact with others.

DAY TWO

REVEALED: SPENDING FOCUSED TIME

After calling His initial five disciples and taking them to the wedding in Cana, Jesus heads back to Jerusalem for the Passover. After He interacts with Nicodemus, we find a simple verse that most people miss. We are told in John 3:22, "After this, Jesus and his disciples went to the Judean countryside, where he spent time with them and baptized" (csb). The word here for "spent time with" is the Greek word that means "getting under the skin of, rub between, or go deeper with."[1] Jesus knew that in order to reveal the Father to His disciples, He first needed to get to know them on a deeper level. And this would take time. Relationships are a two-way process. They needed to get to know Jesus better and Jesus needed to get to know them.

In order to "reveal" the Father to them, why would these relationships be necessary? Think hard about this question. Try to go deeper with it.

> Jesus knew that in order to reveal the Father to His disciples, he first needed to get to know them on a deeper level. And this would take time.

In John 2:1–11, we know Jesus spent a couple of weeks with His initial followers as they made their way up to Galilee (five-day journey), and then went to the wedding with Jesus' brothers and mother. Why might it be valuable for Jesus' disciples to spend time with Jesus' mother and brothers (and maybe relatives who were getting married)?

Read John 2:12. What do you think the discussion was about during these "few days" in Capernaum?

In John 2:13–22, Jesus' disciples see a different side of Jesus when He cleanses the temple. It is interesting to see that the text says that while the Jews "demanded" (v. 18 NLT) the disciples "remembered" (v. 17) and "recalled" (v. 22). What does this tell us about the methods Jesus used in "revealing" His Father to His disciples?

SPENDING MORE TIME WITH NEW BELIEVERS

Who are a couple of relatively new believers the Lord has placed in your life? Write their names below, and then place them in Your Circles on page 173.

List a couple of ways that you could intentionally spend more time with them and seek to "reveal the Father to them."

Intentionally making disciples requires that we learn to take the everyday events of life and use them as opportunities to point people to the heavenly Father, revealing Him. Practical, everyday events can mean simply a shopping trip together, a meal together, or an opportunity to work on a project. List a couple of practical ways in which you have learned to make this happen. What do you need to get better at?

DAY THREE

REVEALED: GOING DEEPER AND CARING ENOUGH TO CONFRONT

One of the surprises I had as I began to study the life of Christ chronologically was the amount of time Jesus spent with a few of His key disciples. Eighteen months into Jesus' ministry, we are told in Matthew 4 and Mark 1, Jesus selects four men (soon five with Matthew). Later He would choose twelve so that He could be with them and "send them out" (Mark 3:14). From this point you find Jesus with the crowds seventeen times, but forty-six times with His few disciples.[2] Jesus chose to go deeper with a few after He challenged them to "follow me, and I will make you fishers of men" (Matt. 4:19 ESV).

As these few men began to travel with Jesus, they had a chance to hear Jesus again and again as He taught. Hearing Him teach in many settings caused a better understanding and surfaced additional questions.

GOING DEEPER

Read Matthew 13:36. What would it have felt like if you were one of the disciples and were able to ask Jesus questions that you might be thinking?

Read Acts 1:3–6. When Jesus appeared to His team of core disciples, do you think that this was encouraging for them? Why or why not?

> From this point you find Jesus with the crowds seventeen times, but forty-six times with His few disciples.

Why is it so important to have someone whom we can ask pressing questions that we may face as we go through life?

Describe who that person is in your life. What is it about that person that makes them so helpful?

What happens to most people if they don't have that type of person?

CARING ENOUGH TO CONFRONT

Read Mark 7:14–23. When Jesus left the crowds and entered the house, Jesus was now with His few disciples. Mark 7:18 literally means: are you so "senseless, foolish, or stupid"?[3] Do you think this stung the disciples? Why did Jesus confront them in this way?

Read Matthew 17:14–20. Do you think this stung Jesus' disciples? Be honest in your answer. Why was Jesus so direct here?

What are you learning about caring enough to confront? Give an example of when you've done this well.

Give an example of when you haven't confronted well. What did you learn from this experience?

GOING DEEPER WITH YOUR FEW

Who are the committed workers (the mature believers who are engaged with you in the harvest field) that the Lord has brought into your life? Write their names below.

What are some ways that you can go deeper with them? Do they most need "grace" or "truth" from you? (Remember, your objective, like Jesus', is to reveal the Father to them.)

REVEALED: EXALTING THE FATHER IN EVERYTHING

In John 17:7, Jesus makes an amazing statement. Write the verse below:

This statement is made after a week of confrontation, crisis, difficulty, and soon-to-be betrayal and crucifixion. This statement mirrors what Jesus said in John 3:21, 5:19a, 5:30a, and what He instructed in John 15:5c. What principle does Jesus model here?

Jesus always exalted His Father in everything. He consistently said that everything we ever do comes from above and that He could "do nothing on [His] own initiative" (John 8:28 NASB). I'm sure that what Jesus stated in John 3:21 is just His paraphrase of Isaiah 26:12, "LORD, you establish peace for us; *all that we have accomplished you have done for us.*"

Would your disciples be able to say this about you—that you are exalting your Father in everything? Why is it critical for our disciples to see this truth modeled?

If we want to grow in our ability to exalt the Father in everything, and thus reveal the Father to those around us, we must practice. What are some practical ways you can begin right away to "exalt the Lord" to your disciples? Try to be very specific.

Express what is in your heart by writing out a prayer to the Father reflecting what you have learned from this week's study.

> Jesus clearly revealed His Father to His disciples.

Jesus clearly revealed His Father to His disciples. He did this by always exalting the Father as the source of everything—acknowledging that everything came from the Father (John 17:7). This is a powerful lesson to learn, as it frees us up to be who we are. It is not about us or our talents; it is about the Father. Even Jesus acknowledged everything as coming from above. That takes the pressure off! We can be vessels through whom the Father works, just as Jesus was!

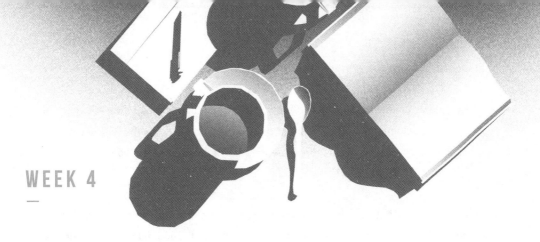

SPEAK: "I GAVE THEM THE WORDS YOU GAVE ME"

(JOHN 17:8)

Go deeper: Watch videos online and download the Like Jesus app. LikeJesus.church/live

GETTING STARTED

In John 17:8, Jesus gives us His second practical priority for making disciples. "For I gave them the words you gave me and they accepted them. They knew with certainty that I came from you, and they believed that you sent me." The Greek word used here for "word" is *rhema* rather than *logos*. *Logos* refers to the whole of Scripture and to the person of Christ, but *rhema*, in most cases, references the spoken Word applied in a unique situation. While this interpretation is debated in many circles, Vine writes in his Expository Dictionary of New Testament Words:

> The significance of rhema (as distinct from logos) is exemplified in the injunction to take "the sword of the Spirit, which is the word of God," Ephesians 6:17; here the reference is not to the whole Bible as such, but to the individual scripture which the Spirit brings to our remembrance for use in time of need, a prerequisite being the regular storing of the mind with Scripture.[1]

Jesus, in His humanity, was clearly a student of the Scriptures. Eighty times in the Gospels, Jesus quotes from more than seventy chapters from twenty-four different Old Testament books. The Word was center stage in Jesus' life and ministry.

As Jesus saw His disciples sharing the good news, He knew His three years of investing in them would now yield the intended fruit of multiplication.

He studied it, knew it, and lived in accordance with it. He accused the Sadducees of ignorance, claiming, "You are in error because you do not know the Scriptures" (Matt. 22:29). On several occasions He challenged His opponents, "Have you never read?" (see Matt. 21:16, 42; 22:31).

Many imagine that, as a little baby, Jesus was downloaded with all biblical data. It did not happen that way. Jesus studied the Word. Even as a young man, Jesus became a student of the Scriptures, increasing "in wisdom and stature, and in favor with God and man" (Luke 2:52). It was His custom to go up to the synagogue to learn and read the Scriptures (Luke 4:16), for zeal for His Father's house consumed Him (John 2:17). As an excellent Jewish boy, at the age of ten Jesus was probably able to quote all of the first five books of the Bible, a skill achieved by many of the top students in the synagogue.

Over forty years ago, when I became a Christian, I didn't even know the difference between the Old and New Testaments. I remember someone asking me to read from the Old Testament, and my response was, "I just have a new Bible, not an old one." Early on as a young Christian, I became discouraged, wondering if I could ever master the whole Bible. But a wise professor in Bible school told me, "Just keep at it, and you will be amazed how God will teach you." Now, forty years later, I find myself with confidence in my ability to "correctly handle[] the word of truth" (2 Tim. 2:15). But it took years of study and a growing willingness to work at it.

Jesus was able to say, "I gave them the words you gave me" (John 17:8), because He was a student of God's Word. Jesus said, "My teaching is not my own. It comes from the one who sent me" (John 7:16). What a statement! Jesus added, "I do nothing on my own but speak just what the Father has taught me" (John 8:28). Jesus was able to impart truth to His disciples because He was a student of the Word.

But not only was Jesus a learner, He was also a good listener. He was able to take the whole of God's Word (*logos*) and through the Spirit apply it to everyday life (*rhema*). As Jesus went through everyday life with His disciples, He was able to say, "For I did not speak on my own, but the Father who sent me commanded me to say all that I have spoken" (John 12:49). He listened well. And then He, in turn, told His disciples that they too could experience this reality, "for the Holy Spirit will teach you at that time what you should say" (Luke 12:12).

Because Jesus listened well, Jesus was able to say, "everything that I learned from my

Jesus, in His humanity, was clearly a student of the Scriptures.

Father I have made known to you" (John 15:15). "What I have heard from him I tell the world" (8:26).

Because Jesus studied the Scriptures and then listened to the Spirit as He went through the everyday events of life with His disciples, He was able to pray in John 17:8, "I gave them the words you gave me." His priority was exactly that: giving to His disciples what the Father had given to Him.

Can you describe a time when God gave you the opportunity to share His words with someone in such a way that you knew it was His Spirit working through you?

What happens if we do not know God's Word well enough to be able to use it? What can we substitute in place of God's Word?

Go back to the Scriptures I quoted above (John 12:49; 15:15; 8:26; 17:8), and look at how clearly they say that Jesus listened to His heavenly Father. What do we need to learn about listening from Jesus? Think this through carefully.

None of us ever feels completely adequate in handling God's Word, but the beauty of God's family and His Spirit is His promise to "guide [us] into all the truth" (John 16:13) and to give us what we need when we need it.

What is the major truth that God has been teaching you lately? What you have been learning is not by accident. God wants you to share with others this truth that He is teaching you. What principles can we learn about our life experiences from 2 Corinthians 1:3–8?

As you study His Word and listen to His Spirit, God wants to work through you. Write below and then share with your group what God is teaching you.

DAY ONE

SPEAKING: PSALM 34

During the next four days, I want to guide you in doing what Jesus did: giving your disciples the words the Father gives you.

Last week, I had you identify some people God has in your life who are seekers, new believers, and then a few workers. Write their names below. As we work through John 17, I'd like to keep referring to these people God has placed in your life. For the purpose of this study, let's refer to them as your disciples that God has brought to you. Some of you might feel uncomfortable calling them your disciples. Remember, in John 13:1, we are told that Jesus "loved his own who were in the world, he loved them to the end." These whom Jesus loved were His disciples. Do you love those God has placed in your life? If so, don't feel uncomfortable calling them your disciples. If God has brought them in your life and you love them with His love, that is what they are.

Who are the "seekers" God has placed in your life? (p. 68)

Who are the new believers God has placed in your life? (p. 70)

Who are the committed workers God has placed in your life? (p. 73)

IN THE MORNING:

Read Psalm 34. Ask God to speak to you through it. Ask Him, by His Spirit, to guide you into truth that speaks to your heart today. This is the *rhema* of God's Word, where His written Word comes alive in your life personally through His Spirit as you face life events. Read and reread, meditating on Psalm 34, until you sense God speaking to you, making His Word alive in your life situation. Listen carefully, and then write down what God gives to you through His Spirit.

Now, very simply, be intentional about doing what Jesus did. He said, "I gave them the words you gave me" (John 17:8).

Think of some simple ways you can share with the people you listed above what God has given to you. Maybe have them over for a cup of coffee, maybe through email, text, or a phone call. Simply say: "Can I share with you something God has shown me today from Psalm 34?" If you can't share today with one of your disciples (loved ones), is there someone else you can share with today?

IN THE EVENING:

How did it go today? Who did you share with? What went well? How can you improve tomorrow?

DAY TWO

SPEAKING: PROVERBS 3

IN THE MORNING:

Today we're reading from a different book of the Bible. Read Proverbs 3. Again, ask God to speak to you through His Word. Ask His Spirit to guide you into truth that will relate to your life situation. Read and reread until you sense His Spirit speaking to you through His Word about something you are facing in your life. Look carefully at the text, listen carefully to what He is saying to you, and then write that word below:

Allow God to use you in the events of your everyday life.

Again today, do what Jesus did: "I gave them the words you gave me" (John 17:8). With whom can you intentionally share what God has shared with you? Be bolder today. Are there others that you can share with? What about at work, or at school, or in the neighborhood? If God has given you something, as you give, you are given even more. Be intentional today. It may simply be with the gas station attendant as you fill up your car with gas. Allow God to use you in the events of your everyday life.

I'd encourage you to simply ask your friends: "Can I share with you something that I have learned today as I read Proverbs 3?" It doesn't need to be profound, just share what you felt God gave to you. It may mean just reading a verse, or making a simple comment about it. Allow God to work. Walk today as Jesus walked, giving away the words He has given you (John 17:8).

Be creative. Have fun.

Ask God to use you. Ask Him for new opportunities to share the words He gave to you. Be open to whatever He brings your way.

IN THE EVENING:

How did it go today? How many people were you able to share with? Be honest—was this easy or hard? Are you getting better at it? What are you learning?

DAY THREE

SPEAKING: ISAIAH 30

By now I imagine you either love this exercise because you have enjoyed sharing with others what God is teaching you, or you have struggled doing this because you didn't feel adequate.

IN THE MORNING:

Let's do this again—at least one more day. Today we will go into another book of the Bible: Isaiah 30. These are isolated chapters of the Old Testament, but they are powerful chapters. I'm sure Jesus was very familiar with each of these books. God can use any passage of Scripture to speak to us; and when He does, we gain by giving it away to others.

Ask God to speak to you today. Read and reread the passage until you sense the Lord saying something specific to you about your life situation. Listen carefully to His Spirit, and then write out what He is saying to you today:

> God can use any passage of Scripture to speak to us; and when He does, we gain by giving it away to others.

Today, be very intentional in your sharing. Go back to the names you wrote down in Day 1, and make an intentional effort to invest your life in these people by giving them a call, writing them an email, or going out to coffee with them. Share with them what God is sharing with you. Invest in them. Be honest, and allow God to give you the words to use. Like Jesus, give them the words the Father has given to you.

IN THE EVENING:

How did it go today? Write below how the experience was. What are you learning through this process? Be honest.

FOR FURTHER THOUGHT:

For a period of two years, I worked hard at training people how to share their faith. We had written a manual on evangelism and took thousands through the training. But when we did some honest evaluation, we found little change in people's behavior. What we found through our evaluation impacted all of our future training in evangelism. We made two simple observations through our research. First, if people were unable to share with fellow Christians what God was teaching them, they rarely, if ever, felt free to share with non-Christians what God had taught them. So the principle was simple: start sharing with fellow Christians what God is teaching you, and evangelism with nonbelievers becomes easier and more natural.

Second, we learned that those who were most effective at sharing their faith were those who talked to non-Christians just as if they were Christians. In other words, when we begin to prejudge people with certain values and beliefs, we begin to speak to them very differently. Those most effective at evangelism and discipling were those who just loved God and loved people and were eager to share what God was teaching them. They talked to non-Christians just as they talked with Christians, honestly sharing what God was doing in their lives. This openness and honesty became a powerful tool in God's hand. Just giving to others what God has given to us is a powerful discipling tool. And as Jesus simply said: "I gave them the words you gave me."

What might change in your life if you began simply to make it a pattern of your life every day to share with others what God is sharing with you? How might this change your view of evangelism?

DAY FOUR

SPEAKING: GOD WANTS TO SPEAK

So far this week, we have seen that God wants to use us to share with others what He is teaching us. Discipling like Jesus is simply passing on to others the lessons we are learning. Jesus said so clearly: "I gave them the words you gave me" (John 17:8). This was the pattern of His life.

God truly delights in speaking to His children. He longs to be gracious to them and reveal His plan to them. He delights in leading His children along the path of life and clearly wants to reveal His plans to them. Look up the following verses and discover what they tell us about God's desire to speak to us and lead us into His plans and truth.

Read Amos 3:7 and 4:13. What do these verses tell us about God's desires?

> Discipling like Jesus is simply passing on to others the lessons we are learning.

Read Proverbs 3:32. What amazing truth can we learn about God in this verse? What does it mean that God "takes the upright into his confidence"?

Read Isaiah 28:23 and 26. What do these verses tell us about God?

Read Isaiah 30:20–21. What does this tell us about listening to the voice of God?

What did Jesus say about the words He gave to His disciples in the following verses?

John 7:16

John 14:24

Read John 16:13–15. What did Jesus now say would happen to His disciples? Why is this such a valuable resource in this fast-changing world?

What an amazing gift God has given us through His Holy Spirit! You may want to just stop, take a moment, and thank the Holy Spirit for guiding you into truth.

What was the admonition to the New Testament church in the following verses in Revelation? (Read Revelation 2:7, 11, 17, 29; 3:6, 13, 22 and write out what these verses mean to you.)

God wants to speak to us. He wants to guide us into all truth. He has promised to reveal to us, through His Spirit and written Word, His truth for our lives. But as He gives to us, He wants us to give to others. It is in giving that we receive. Discipling like Jesus means that, like Jesus, we pass on to our disciples the truths that God gives to us.

From this simple truth presented in this week's study from John 17:8, what are your next steps to becoming more like Jesus in this area? Be specific.

PRAYER: "I PRAY FOR THEM"

(JOHN 17:9)

Go deeper: Watch videos online and download the Like Jesus app. LikeJesus.church/live

GETTING STARTED

Jesus' ministry began and ended with prayer. Scripture tells us that at the beginning of His ministry "as he was praying" (Luke 3:21), the Spirit came upon Him. At the end of His ministry, as He hung on the cross, the very last words uttered by Jesus was a prayer: "Father, into your hands I commit my spirit." At that moment, the centurion praised God, saying, "Surely this was a righteous man" (Luke 23:46–47).

Jesus launched His disciple-making mission by spending forty days in fasting and prayer. Coming out of this intense time of prayer, Jesus goes back to where John was baptizing and begins to call His disciples to "come and see" and "follow me" (John 1:39 NCV, 43). There are over thirty-three different instances in the Gospels that speak of Jesus praying for His disciples.

It should then be no surprise to us that the very last thing Jesus will do with His disciples is to gather them around Him and pray with and for them. Just before His betrayal in Gethsemane, He allows His disciples to listen in on His prayer for them. "I pray for them," Jesus states, "I am not praying for the world, but for those you have given me, for they are yours" (John 17:9).

As the Master Discipler, Jesus knew that prayer was a nonnegotiable discipline. How many times did He agonize in prayer for them? How many times did He ask for the

Father to protect them, keep them, and teach them? How many times did He seek His Father's wisdom for what they needed next? Why did they seem so slow to learn? For their lack of insight? How many times did Jesus give thanks for them, like He did so many times here in this final prayer?

Perhaps one of the major reasons Jesus spent so much time in prayer for His disciples was because of how He regarded them.

We often think of Jesus as the Father's gift to us, and that He is. But here in John 17, we see Jesus stating that His disciples and their disciples (John 17:20) are the Father's gift to Him (John 17:2, 6, 9, 24). What a thought! We are God's gift to Jesus. What an amazing perspective Jesus had. What a grateful heart He displays to His Father in prayer. Write out these verses below, because doing so can help us appreciate each word of Scripture:

John 17:2

John 17:6

John 17:9

John 17:24

What changes in our attitudes when we begin to think of ourselves as the Father's "love gift" to His Son? How did this attitude impact Jesus' attitude toward His disciples?

Another way to view ourselves as God's "love gift" to His Son is to realize that, as believers, we are the bride of Christ. God *gave us* to Jesus as His bride. As that bride, look at these verses and describe what this bridal relationship is like. What are the key elements of that bridal relationship?

Ephesians 5:25–27

Revelation 19:7–9

Isaiah 62:3, 5

PRAYING FOR SEEKERS

When Jesus was twelve, He spent three days in the temple, and when His parents finally found Him, Mary asked Him: "Son, why have you treated us like this? Your father and I have been anxiously searching for you" (Luke 2:48). After this event, we are told that Jesus "went down to Nazareth with them and was obedient to them. But his mother treasured all these things in her heart" (Luke 2:51).

For approximately eighteen years in Nazareth, Jesus "learned obedience from what he suffered" (Heb. 5:8). Without sin, He grew His obedience muscles through what He suffered. One day, His cousin John comes preaching in the region of the Jordan in the power of Elijah. Soon word begins to spread, as he is proclaiming that he is not the Messiah but that the Messiah is coming and he is not worthy to untie His sandals (John 1:26–27).

Back in the small village of Nazareth, Jesus served faithfully for many years in the marketplace as a master craftsman (we often translate the Greek word *tekton* as "carpenter"). Since we no longer hear about Joseph, most assume Joseph has passed away, and Jesus is serving as the head of the home with Mary and His four brothers and several sisters (Matt. 13:55–56).

I can easily imagine Jesus one morning, having time alone with His Father, sitting on the Nazareth ridge overlooking the Jezreel Valley. The Spirit speaks to Him and tells Him, "today is the day—go and get baptized by your cousin John." Traveling the five-day journey, Jesus goes to Bethany on the other side of the Jordan and has John baptize Him. The heavens are "torn open" and the "Spirit descend(s) on him." The Father boldly proclaims, "You are my Son, whom I love; with you I am well pleased" (Mark 1:10–11).

We are then told that Jesus is thrust into the wilderness by the Spirit, where for forty days He is led about and tempted (Matt. 4:1–11; Mark 1:12–13). He then returned "full of the Holy Spirit" to where John was baptizing, and begins His ministry by calling His first disciples (Luke 4:1).

> For approximately eighteen years in Nazareth, Jesus "learned obedience through what he suffered" (Heb. 5:8).

During those forty days in the wilderness, do you envision Jesus praying about His ministry to come and His first disciples? If so, what do you think He prayed for?

Andrew and John were the very first disciples to approach Jesus. When they did, He asked them, "What do you want?" (John 1:38) Do you think it's possible Andrew and John approached Jesus because He had been praying for disciples in the wilderness period? Explain your answer and why this is important to us.

Do you think it was a coincidence that the very next day (John 1:43) Jesus goes and finds Philip (who was from the same town as Andrew and Peter) and then Philip goes and finds Nathaniel? This may seem like a simple rhetorical question, but think it through. Do you think Jesus had prayed about who He should disciple? Do you think that Jesus may have prayed specifically that the Father would show Him the people He should invest in?

I believe that Jesus, in the wilderness before He launched His ministry, prayed very intentionally for the people His Father wanted Him to invest in. In the same way, if we want to disciple like Jesus, we too need to ask the Father to bring us key people to disciple. Jesus said, "I pray for them . . . those you have given me" (John 17:9). What are the practical implications of this truth in your own life today? Think carefully about your answer.

DAY TWO

PRAYING FOR BELIEVERS

During the second year of His ministry, Jesus had taken His new disciples to a wedding feast in Cana, cleansed the temple during the Passover (John 2), spoken to Nicodemus at night (John 3), traveled through Samaria (John 4), and then returned for a Jewish festival where He clearly presents Himself as the Messiah (John 5).

Returning to Galilee, He presents Himself in His hometown; and after the crowds are "amazed at the gracious words that came from his lips," they soon decide to "throw him off the cliff" (Luke 4:16–30). With John the Baptist being put in prison, Jesus decides to move to Capernaum and begins to go deeper with a handful of disciples. He expands His challenge to four of them (later Matthew is added to this "starting five") to "follow me, and I will make you fishers of men" (Matt. 4:18–22 ESV). Immediately He begins to train them to fish for men by taking them to the synagogue where He heals the demon-possessed man, and then to Peter's home where He heals Peter's mother-in-law, and then ministers to the crowds of Capernaum when word spreads (Mark 1:21–34).

After a full day of ministry in the busy town of Capernaum, Jesus awoke "very early in the morning, while it was still dark, . . . and went off to a solitary place, where he prayed" (Mark 1:35).

What do you think Jesus prayed about that morning? Put yourselves in Jesus' shoes and think deeply about the situation.

How do you think Jesus prayed for His disciples that morning? Again, think intently about this, putting yourself in Jesus' situation.

Earlier we learned that Jesus said, "I gave them the words you gave me" (John 17:8). What words did Jesus give His disciples that morning when they finally found Him and were probably upset with Him because "Everyone [was] looking for [Him]!" (Mark 1:37)?

In His humanity, do you think Jesus may have even been surprised by these words that His Father gave Him? If the whole town was looking for you, wouldn't you immediately think this is God's will for your life today?

Jesus obviously was spending time that morning, praying for His Father's leading and for the Father's will concerning His disciples. What lessons can we learn from this story by how Jesus Himself said, "I pray for them" (John 17:9)?

Why do you think it was important for Jesus' disciples to hear Jesus say that He must go to the other cities and towns? Because the Gospels record these stories, the disciples obviously traveled with Jesus. What do you think the disciples personally needed from this experience?

Do you think Jesus often prayed in this way, seeking wisdom for next steps with His disciples? Try to think creatively and write out what Jesus' prayer may have sounded like.

DAY THREE

PRAYING FOR COMMITTED WORKERS

Jesus often spoke on the importance of prayer. List some of the times you remember Jesus speaking about prayer.

(See Matt. 6:5–8; Matt. 7:7–11; Mark 9:29; etc.)

Luke 9:18 tells us that "when Jesus was praying in private and his disciples were with him," Jesus then asked them a series of questions. What do you think Jesus was praying about during this prayer time? Do you think His prayers and His questions had any correlation? What would be important for us to learn from this as we pray for our disciples?

In Luke 11:1, Jesus' disciples came to Him and asked, "Lord, teach us to pray." It is obvious that those closest to Jesus knew that what made Him different from every other leader was His prayer life! They didn't say, "Lord, teach us to do miracles," or "teach us to teach." They said, "Lord, teach us to pray."

What do you think it was about Jesus' discipline of prayer that caused His disciples to ask this?

What would your disciples need to see in you to want to ask you a similar question?

Read Hebrews 7:25. What does this tell us about Jesus' prayer life today?

Read Romans 8:26–28. In what specific ways does the Holy Spirit help us?

It has been said that if you want to make anyone feel guilty, just talk about prayer! No matter how much we pray, we can often feel we need to pray more. As you think about how Jesus prayed for His disciples, what is encouraging to you in this journey of becoming more like Jesus in the area of prayer for your disciples?

DAY FOUR

PRAYING: PRIORITIZING YOUR DISCIPLES IN PRAYER

On the northern shore of the Sea of Galilee, about five hundred feet above the water level, is a small beautiful cave called Eremos Cave. No larger than ten feet wide, six feet high, and ten feet deep, it received its name from tradition as the place where Jesus may have gone to pray. *Eremos* is the Greek work for "lonely, solitary, quiet, or deserted." Used fifty times in the New Testament, it was the word used in Luke 5:16 when it says Jesus "often withdrew to *eremos* places and prayed."

While we have no proof that this is the place that Jesus came to pray, it has definitely become one of my favorite places in Israel. Its beautiful view of the Sea of Galilee and the surrounding area makes it an enjoyable place to pray. During my last trip to Israel, I was able to spend nine hours in this small cave, reliving an experience from Jesus' ministry.

In Mark 6, when we study Jesus' life chronologically, we see Jesus calling His twelve disciples to Himself and sending them out two by two. A number of events are happening simultaneously. At the same time Jesus is sending out His disciples, we are also told of a birthday party at Tiberius for Herod Antipas. Here, in his foolishness, Herod promises the head of John the Baptist to the daughter of Herodias.

Also during this time, the disciples begin to return from their trips and report to Jesus all that they saw God doing. They are full of joy. During this report session, Jesus also gets word of John's beheading (Matt. 14:12), and Jesus seeks to slip away with His disciples (Mark 6:31).

As they are seeking to get away, the crowd sees them depart and run together on foot along the shore. Jesus, seeing the crowd and knowing their need, stops and ministers to them and ends up feeding the five thousand gathered who were without food. During this time, Jesus also gets a report that the crowd "intended to come and make him king by force" (John 6:15). He made His disciples get into the boat and go to the safe side of Bethsaida, away from Herod Antipas's reach. Dismissing the crowd, we are told that Jesus "went up on a mountainside by himself to pray" (Matt. 14:23). Because we know it was about sunset when this happened—and that Jesus would come walking to His disciples on the waters at about 3 a.m.—we can deduce from the story that Jesus would spend about nine hours that night in prayer.

In light of all the events that happened that day, what do you think Jesus prayed about during those nine hours?

Do you think Jesus needed to pray about the impact of John's death? Why or why not?

What about the crowds who wanted to make Jesus king? How do you think Jesus prayed for them?

What about His own feelings, since He was not allowed to free John from prison? (He knew the Messiah came to set the prisoners free. See Luke 4:18 and compare with Luke 7:22–23. Notice the omission of "proclaim freedom for the prisoners" and "set the oppressed free"). How do you think this impacted Jesus—and maybe even Jesus' family?

What do you think He prayed for concerning His disciples who were still "straining at the oars" (Mark 6:48)?

Jesus made prayer for His disciples one of His major concerns. What happens when we fail to pray for those in whom we are investing? (See 1 Sam. 12:23.)

Summarize, in your own words, the major reason why your prayer is so critical for your disciples. What lessons have you learned from Jesus?

Take a moment right now to stop and pray for those whom the Lord has placed in your life that He wants you to disciple. Write their names down and what you are praying for them.

PROTECT: "WHILE I WAS WITH THEM, I PROTECTED THEM AND KEPT THEM SAFE"

(JOHN 17:12)

Go deeper: Watch videos online and download the Like Jesus app. LikeJesus.church/live

GETTING STARTED

When my daughters were young, I felt a great burden to protect them. They often ran to their mom when they needed some mercy, but they would run to me when they were afraid.

In an attempt to keep them safe, we baby-proofed our home by removing anything that could be dangerous. We placed locks on the doors and locks on the cabinets. We bought furniture with soft cushions and round corners. We constantly watched them, making sure nothing could bring them harm. As they grew up, we carefully directed their friendships and places of play. We stayed away from dangerous places where they could get sick or places where they might be injured. We taught them how to be careful in their actions.

But no matter how hard we tried, evil still entered their world. Broken friendships. Disappointments. Painful experiences. We could not protect them from everything. So often when I think of God's protection, I want nothing of harm to come our way. Even

Christ's protection became like a fortress for His disciples, surrounding them and keeping them safe.

103

today, I want my daughters to be shielded from all problems, all hardships, all evil. But that is impossible.

Jesus sought to protect His disciples in many of the same ways. But He did it perfectly. Through His actions, His prayers, His teachings, His spiritual guidance and provisions, Jesus could say, "While I was with them, I protected them and kept them safe by that name you gave me. None has been lost except the one doomed to destruction so that Scripture would be fulfilled" (John 17:12). He also prayed, "I am coming to you. Holy Father, protect them by the power of your name" (v. 11).

Jesus used two words here in John 17 to describe the protection He gave. In the NIV the first word (*tereo*) is translated "protect" and the second word (*phylasso*) is translated "kept." Both words have similar meanings: to guard, observe carefully, keep a close watch upon, to care for. The first word is used of a military term such as a fortress. Christ's protection became like a fortress for His disciples, surrounding them and keeping them safe.

As the Good Shepherd, Jesus knew this was His role. Read John 10:11–18 and list the ways a good shepherd protects his sheep.

How does the hired hand act?

In ancient Israel, a shepherd would often lie across the entrance of the pen at night, and anyone entering the sheep pen would have to go past the shepherd. This provided a sense of security for the sheep. How does the Good Shepherd define His protection of His sheep in John 10:7–10?

How does the Good Shepherd define His protection of His sheep in John 10:27–30?

List the different ways the Good Shepherd protects His sheep in Psalm 23.

As you think about the incarnate Jesus, list some other ways in which you felt Jesus protected His disciples. Try to be specific.

DAY ONE

PROTECTION THROUGH TEACHING

In the "come and see" phase, Jesus taught how people needed to "enter" into His kingdom (John 3:5) by being born again. John preached, "Repent, for the kingdom of heaven has come near" (Matt. 3:2) and when John was put in prison, Jesus then picked up that preaching (Matt. 4:17). The Bible records over thirty-three things that happen to us the moment we pass from darkness to light, from an enemy of God to a friend.[1] Our lives are transformed, and we enter into God's protective care as His children (John 1:12). This is a spiritual protection from above.

In the "follow me" phase, the word "follow" means to line up behind and learn of someone. Often used as a discipling word to call new disciples, it called the disciple to walk in the discipler's footsteps and learn from him. Through the teaching and modeling of the discipler's life, disciples are directed into safe paths. This is a relational protection offered to those in close proximity.

But in the next phase, "follow me, and I will make you fishers of men" (Matt. 4:19 ESV), you now find Jesus being much more direct in His teaching. He begins to clearly warn them as He teaches them. Read the following passages and list some of these warnings:

Matthew 5:11–13

Matthew 6:19–21

> The Bible records over thirty-three things that happen to us the moment we pass from darkness to light, from an enemy of God to a friend.

When Jesus sent His disciples out two by two, He gave them a number of warnings. Read the following passages and list some of these warnings:

Matthew 10:16–31

How do you think the disciples received these warnings? Do you think any of the disciples felt they really didn't need any of this teaching? What would have been their attitude?

Do you think these warnings helped the disciples prepare as they went out two by two? In what ways?

PROTECTION THROUGH CAREFUL OBSERVATIONS

A good shepherd always watches carefully over his sheep.

My wife and I care deeply for our three daughters. We watched how our girls interacted with each other and with outsiders. We noticed carefully how they talked with people, what they said, and how they responded to all types of people. We carefully (remember, the word for "protect" means to attend to carefully) watched our daughters' interactions and actions to help them grow into maturity.

Through the seemingly small interactions of life, Jesus was carefully watching over His disciples—watching how they were interacting with each other and with the truths Jesus was presenting.

If our daughters didn't look people in the eye when they talked to them, we told them and made them practice looking directly at people. If they failed to be thankful, we'd correct them and give them opportunities to write thank you notes. If they were disrespectful of elders, they heard strongly from us and would have to go and ask forgiveness. We constantly monitored our daughters' actions to guide them in their people and life skills.

Can you think of some ways Jesus protected His disciples by watching over their actions and interactions?

Read Luke 9:46–48. What were the disciples arguing about? How did Jesus address this?

Read Luke 22:24–27. What were the disciples disputing about here? How does this dispute differ from the Luke 9 passage? Look closely. Jesus noticed the details.

Read the parallel story in Matthew 20:20–28. Notice how the disciples were responding to each other. What did Jesus do to address this issue?

Through the seemingly small interactions of life, Jesus was carefully watching over His disciples—watching how they were interacting with each other and with the truths Jesus was presenting. In the story recorded in Matthew 20:20–28, what could have been the negative outcomes if the disciples did not learn the lesson well?

As you think about your disciples, the people God has brought into your life to invest in, how are their interactions with each other, with their spouse, with outsiders? Part of protecting your disciples is caring enough to lovingly confront them in the interactions of life. Are there any discussions you need to have with your disciples?

DAY THREE

PROTECTION THROUGH OUR ACTIONS

Do you remember the story last week about Jesus going to Eremos Cave and spending nine hours in prayer after He commanded His disciples to go on ahead of Him to Bethsaida? The text is even more direct. It says, "Immediately Jesus made his disciples get into the boat and go on ahead of him to Bethsaida, while he dismissed the crowd" (Mark 6:45). There was a reason for this.

Herod Antipas had just beheaded John the Baptist. The crowds were furious and five thousand men gathered and ran along the shore, wanting to take Jesus by force and make Him king (John 6:15). Herod knew about this. The region was small and Herod surely had his spies in the crowd. Jesus knew it was not safe to stay in the area, so He made His disciples go on ahead of Him to the safe side, where Bethsaida was, in Philip Antipas's territory. Jesus was concerned, I believe, for the physical safety of His disciples.

Would you agree with me that during this evening of prayer in Mark 6:45–46, Jesus exhibited genuine concern for His disciples? Why or why not?

Soon after this event, Jesus took His disciples out of the region to the far regions of Tyre and Sidon, and then all the way north to Caesarea Philippi. The crowds were becoming dangerous and the tension was mounting. It wasn't time yet for Jesus to make His final approach into Jerusalem. There was much more the disciples needed to learn. I believe He was concerned for their safety, as much as He was concerned that they learn all that they needed to know.

John 17:12 states that "None has been lost except the one doomed to destruction so that Scripture would be fulfilled." Judas was that person. When were the seeds of destruction planted in Judas's life, causing him to want to betray Jesus? We may never know. The Scriptures tell us that Jesus "knew who was going to betray him" (John 13:11) and in the upper room, Jesus was deeply "troubled in spirit" (13:21) and told him, "What you are about to do, do quickly" (13:27).

But I've often wondered if the tiny details recorded in Matthew 10:2–4 might give us a clue.

Have you ever wondered, when Jesus sent out His disciples two by two, giving them "authority to drive out impure spirits and to heal every disease and sickness" (Matt. 10:1), who got paired up to go out with Judas?

As someone who has sent hundreds of people out two by two to do evangelism, I have always noticed that some, out of fear, never get around to sharing their faith. They often just end up talking with themselves rather than taking time to share their faith. Could this have been the situation with Judas, when he was sent out two by two? While we may not know who got paired up with Judas in Matthew 10, the text seems to give us a clue. In this passage, the Twelve are lumped together into twos: Simon and Andrew, James and John, Philip and Bartholomew, Thomas and Matthew, James and Thaddaeus, Simon the Zealot and Judas Iscariot (the one who betrayed Him).

> I believe He was concerned for their safety, as much as He was concerned that they learn all that they needed to know.

Maybe the one zealot among the Twelve who was eagerly waiting for the Messiah to conquer the Romans planted seeds of doubt in Judas Iscariot that Jesus was never going to make the move against Rome. Maybe, in that last week leading up to Jerusalem, when everyone sensed that a confrontation was coming, maybe Judas, due to his discussions with the zealot, also concluded that Jesus was never going to take on the Romans.

We don't know, and this is simply speculation. But could Jesus have even carefully managed the details of His disciples to such a degree as pairing up Simon the Zealot with Judas Iscariot? Speculation, yes. But Jesus was a master shepherd who carefully observed His disciples in all the details of life.

Look closely at John 18:1–9. How was Jesus carefully seeking to protect His disciples, even in the garden? (See specifically verse 9.)

Jesus revealed the Father to His disciples. He gave them the words His Father gave Him. He prayed for them and worked carefully to protect them—and none perished except the son of destruction.

Is there an issue in your disciple's life that you need to address out of concern and genuine love for them? If so, identify that issue below:

As clearly as you possibly can, identify exactly what that issue is that you need to discuss with your disciple. Clearly name the disciple and the issue involved. Ask God for wisdom to discern when and how to address this issue. Think through the various possible ways they might respond. Pray for wisdom and clarity, and then make an appointment to talk through the issue with your disciple. Be honest and ask first for permission to share a concern. Allow God's Spirit time to bring resolution to the concern.

DAY FOUR

PROTECTION THROUGH OUR PROMISES

Perhaps the most significant way in which Jesus protected His disciples is mentioned in His prayer on two different occasions. John 17:11 says, "Holy Father, protect them by the power of your name," and then again in verse 12 He says, "I protected them and kept them safe by that name you gave me."

Many different conclusions have been drawn by the reference to that "name." Some have tried to tie it to the "I am" statements of Jesus; others have tied it to the very name *Jesus*. However, the "name of the Lord" almost always refers to the entirety of God's character and conduct. Proverbs 18:10 says it so well, "The name of the Lord is a fortified tower; the righteous run to it and are safe."

> It is the whole character of God that makes us safe.

It is the whole character of God that makes us safe. Throughout this whole prayer of Jesus, we find that protection. Look at some of the verses in this prayer alone that speak of our security in Christ. Underline key phrases that speak of our protection in Christ because of His promises:

John 17, verse 2: "For you granted him authority over all people that he might give eternal life to all those you have given him."

Verse 6: "They were yours; you gave them to me."

Verse 11: "I am coming to you. Holy Father, protect them by the power of your name, the name you gave me, so that they may be one as we are one."

Verse 16: "They are not of the world, even as I am not of it."

Verse 21: ". . . Father just as you are in me and I am in you. May they also be in us."

Verses 22–23: "I have given them the glory that you gave me, that they may be one as we are one—I in them and you in me."

Verse 23–24: ". . . you sent me and have loved them even as you have loved me. Father, I want those you have given me to be with me where I am, and to see my glory."

Verse 26: "I . . . will continue to make you known in order that the love you have for me may be in them and that I myself may be in them."

What about God's character gives you confidence that you are secure in Him?

In John 10:25–30 Jesus lists at least several very dogmatic promises to His sheep. List them.

How eternal is eternal? Jesus said He gave them eternal life.

When Jesus said, "They shall never perish; no one will snatch them out of my hand," do you think He meant it?

When Jesus said, "My Father . . . is greater than all," does this say anything about His character (name)?

In Matthew 28:16–20, Jesus also gives us one final, powerful promise. Look at the last part of verse 20. This is an imperative command to look closely at Him (the word translated "surely" or "behold" is a command). What promise does He give us here?

This phrase can literally be translated: "the whole of every moment, I will be with you." What a great promise for His eternal spiritual protection.

As you think of how Jesus could pray, "I protected them . . . by that name you gave me" (John 17:12), what does this look like as you work with your disciples? How can you help them appreciate the promises that Jesus offers to those who are His?

Stop right now and pray for those God has brought into your life to disciple. Pray that they would sense God's protecting promises. And also, at the same time, pray that they would sense your loving care for them as someone who, like Jesus, could say, "I protected them" (knowing that ultimately all of us are in the hands of Jesus for His ultimate care and protection).

SENT: "AS YOU SENT ME INTO THE WORLD, I HAVE SENT THEM INTO THE WORLD"

(JOHN 17:18)

Go deeper: Watch videos online and download the Like Jesus app. LikeJesus.church/live

GETTING STARTED

God is a sending God. And each of us is His "sent one."

The "sent-ness" of Jesus captures the very essence of who God is. Jesus was "sent" because God is a sending God. Jesus sent His disciples because Jesus too is a sending Savior. Sending has been His heart and nature from the very beginning.

Over forty times in the gospel of John, Jesus tells us that His Father sent Him! For Jesus to state over forty times that He has been sent, what does this tell us about Jesus' mindset?

Jesus' attitude about His "sent-ness" is clear in so many of His statements. Let's look at a few of these verses in the book of John and see how in His teaching, Jesus emphasizes the importance of His "sent-ness." Write down the unique point Jesus was making in each verse:

John 4:34

John 5:24

Jesus was "sent" because God is a sending God. Jesus sent His disciples, because Jesus too is a sending Savior.

John 5:30

John 6:29

John 6:38

John 7:33

John 8:29

From just these verses, why do you think Jesus' "sent-ness" was so important to Him?

In John 17, in six different verses where Jesus is talking with His heavenly Father, Jesus references His "sent-ness."

Read John 17 and write out these six passages: vv. 3, 8, 18, 21, 23, 25. Why do you think Jesus, in His final prayer for His disciples, puts such a major emphasis on His being "sent"?

In John 17:18, Jesus makes this clarifying statement, "As you sent me into the world, I have sent them into the world." Jesus clearly states that He has sent His disciples, "just as" He was sent. As you initially think about this, what are some of the ways in which we are sent "just as" Jesus was sent?

DAY ONE

SENDING IN THE WHOLE OF SCRIPTURE

We tend to think of missionary activity only as a New Testament activity. But God is the author of mission. The word "mission" is from a Latin word meaning "to send." In both the Old Testament and the New Testament, God is a missionary God.

In Genesis 1, after God created man, we are told, "God blessed them and said to them, 'Be fruitful and increase in number; fill the earth and subdue it'" (Gen. 1:28). God's agenda from the very beginning was for man to spread out and multiply over the face of the earth (to be sent). In Genesis 11, after the judgment of the flood, humans gathered and built a tower in an attempt to "make a name for" themselves and not "be scattered over the face of the whole earth" (Gen. 11:4). But God's plan cannot be thwarted. God confused the languages and "the Lord scattered them from there over all the earth" (Gen. 11:8).

In Genesis 12 God called Abraham and sent him to Canaan—the Promised Land for God's people. God blessed Abraham and sent him to be a blessing to all the nations. Blessed to be a blessing.

Jonah was sent (Jonah 1:2). Jonah initially resisted being sent, but finally went. Isaiah was sent. Isaiah was asked, "Whom shall I send? And who will go for us?" Isaiah responded, "Here am I. Send me!" (Isa. 6:8). God has always been a sending God, because God is a God of mission. He is always looking for those who will willingly say, "Send me."

God eventually sent His Son Jesus into the world (John 3:16) to redeem His people and save them from their sin. Jesus consistently and constantly emphasized His "sent-ness." It impacted the way He lived. It impacted His priorities. It impacted the decisions He made. Jesus clearly was aware of and meditated upon the fact that He was "sent."

As He developed His disciples, He eventually appointed twelve of them and called them

> In both the Old Testament and the New Testament, God is a missionary God.

"apostles," which means "sent ones." This very word, *apostolos*, was the same word Jesus used over and over again to describe who He was, the sent one—sent from the Father. He chose them so "that they might be with him and that he might send them out" (Mark 3:14).

Over and over again Jesus prioritized these disciples and equipped them to be sent. Here in John 17 we are told how Jesus prioritized these twelve men, all for the purpose of sending them: "As you sent me into the world, I have sent them into the world" (v. 18). In John 20:21 Jesus restates this truth, "As the Father has sent me, I am sending you."

This is where we, as disciples, now enter into the greater story of God.

We, too, are sent into the world to make disciples in the same way that God sent Jesus and Jesus sent His disciples. God sent His Holy Spirit to empower us to do this. John 14:26 says, "But the Advocate, the Holy Spirit, whom the Father will send in my name, will teach you all things and will remind you of everything I have said to you."

God is a sending God. This has always been the nature and character of God. This has never changed. In Matthew 28:16–20 Jesus said, "Go and make disciples of all nations." We are now the sent ones!

What changes in our life when we begin to think of ourselves as the "sent ones"? Be specific. How will this affect your actions today?

> God is a sending God. This has always been the nature and character of God.

Being sent was a big deal to Jesus. What would happen in our life if we viewed our "sent-ness" with the same priority and focus that Jesus did?

Howard Snyder says, "Church people think about how to get people into the church; kingdom people think about how to get the church into the world. Church people worry that the world might change the church; kingdom people work to see the church change the world."[1] If we are just content to be "saved" but don't appreciate our "sent-ness," what does our life eventually become like?

Pause right now, and ask God to help you live more as a "sent one."

DAY TWO

THE PRIVILEGE OF BEING SENT

Being on mission with God is one of the greatest privileges in all the world.

Because Jesus was sent, He added humanity to His deity, becoming the firstborn of all creation to enter into heaven with a resurrected heavenly body. Because of what Jesus did on the cross, He redeemed a people unto Himself. He acquired a bride called the church, and received even greater glory because of His obedience. He launched His kingdom, an eternal kingdom, in which He will rule as King of kings and Lord of lords and we, as His bride, will rule and reign with Him.

Because Jesus was willing to be sent, He changed the eternal destiny of this fallen world. Being on mission with God provided an eternal blessing for Jesus. It should be a privilege for us also.

Imagine living a life with absolutely no purpose at all. Imagine not knowing where you came from. Imagine not knowing where you are going. Imagine not knowing why you are here. Do you know anyone like that?

Pretend for a while that this is your life. Without meaning, without direction, without destiny. What would that feel like? Try to describe it.

> Being on mission with God provided an eternal blessing for Jesus. It should be a privilege for us also.

Most people can't stand to live this way very long, so they create their own meaning. They create a purpose for which to give their life. What are some of these man-made purposes that, at times, you have created to make life seem meaningful?

As Christ followers, we have the privilege of joining God in His mission. But unfortunately, most of us approach this mission half-heartedly.

Most of us do not live meaningless lives. But neither do we live lives fully appreciating the significance of our "sent-ness." We are somewhere between meaninglessness and meaningful activity. We've learned to navigate the "I'm committed, but not too much" lifestyle. "I've got meaning, but I'm not a fool for Christ." Some days we feel so purposeful; other days we wonder if it is all really worth it. We have become good churchgoers and good people, but definitely not radical for Jesus. We have become really good at walking the fine line between the two realities. As a result, we fail to fully experience the great privilege of being on mission with God.

What would your life look like if it were fully committed to being "sent" just like Jesus was "sent"? What would change?

Think today about how the disciples' lives were impacted when, filled with the Holy Spirit and then in just two and a half years, they "filled Jerusalem with [their] teaching" (Acts 5:28). How did their "sent-ness" take on a new front seat in their lives? What changed in their day-to-day living?

DAY THREE

THE COSTS OF BEING SENT

As we have found out, God is a sending God. It is His very nature and character. He is on mission and wants us to be the same. But it is important to take some time to describe terms.

"Mission" comes from the Latin word for "sent ones." While it does not describe *how* we are sent, it describes *that* we are sent. Mission is what describes the heart of God. God is the source of mission. God has a mission and is on a mission. He sends us to accomplish His mission: the redemption of His creation.

"Missions," on the other hand, is the activity of God's people (the church) to proclaim and demonstrate the kingdom of God in the world. It is what the church seeks to do to live out our mission.

> Mission is what describes the heart of God. God is the source of mission. God has a mission and is on a mission.

"Missional" is a new term often used to describe a way of living. Missional is normally used to describe a directing of our lives to more accurately demonstrate our "sent-ness." We live missionally when we can say, "I'm living a life that is shaped by God's mission." Living as sent ones should shape the way we live.

The word "missionary," however, is usually reserved to describe a Christ follower who senses God's calling on their life to go cross-culturally and take the gospel "to the nations." In one sense, all Christians are called to be missionaries where they live; but normally this term is reserved for those who choose to go cross-culturally because of God's call to make disciples of "all nations." (The Greek word here in Matthew 28:19 is the word *ethnos*, which means "people groups" or "nations.")

Many churches can be very missions minded but not particularly missional. They can be very active in supporting missionaries, sending money overseas, or even going temporarily to help with missionary work. But sending money or missionaries doesn't necessarily make us missional in our lifestyles. God wants both: missions-minded groups of believers who are living missionally. This is the calling of Jesus' prayer in John 17, "As you sent me into the world, I have sent them into the world" (v. 18).

There is a great privilege and reward in living a missional life, but there are also great costs. Perhaps this is why many choose not to live this way. Let's take a moment to think through some of those costs.

As you think about Jesus' life, what did it cost Him when the Scriptures tell us He "became flesh and made his dwelling among us" (John 1:14; see also Phil. 2:6–8)?

As Jesus continued His ministry, what are some of the other costs He faced? Look at these verses and write down those costs:

Matthew 16:21–23

Mark 3:20–21

John 6:66–70

John 7:1

John 7:3–5

John 8:40–41, 48

Living with purpose (sent-ness) is God's calling upon our life. But it is not easy.[2] However, the rewards are far greater than the costs. When we walk as Jesus walked, living missionally, we store up gold, silver, and precious stones (1 Cor. 3:12). But when we live for ourselves, it is wood, hay, and straw, all to be burned up when tested, for the "fire will test the quality of each person's work" (1 Cor. 3:13). Paul understood this when he said, "For our light and momentary troubles are achieving for us an eternal glory that far outweighs them all" (2 Cor. 4:17).

Take a moment to stop and ask the God of mission to help you live a life more in line with our true "sent-ness." Write out in one sentence that prayer to the Lord.

DAY FOUR

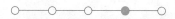

SENT LIKE JESUS

So far in this study of Jesus' prayer in John 17 we have tried to appreciate the passion and emotion with which Jesus prayed for His disciples just before He goes into the garden of Gethsemane to be betrayed. We have also tried to look closer at Jesus' prayer and capture, in His own words, what He said He did to make disciples who could make disciples.

So far we have studied five of those disciplines. First, Jesus stated, "I have revealed you to those whom you gave me" (v. 6). With grace and truth, Jesus entered into this world and exalted His Father in every aspect of His life. So far in this study, what does that say to you about what you need to do to disciple like Jesus discipled? Be specific:

Second, Jesus went on and said in verse 8, "I gave them the words you gave me, and they accepted them." Jesus studied the Scriptures and listened to the Spirit to share with His disicples what the Father revealed to Him. What does that look like in your life? What does that mean for you personally?

Next, in verse 9, Jesus said, "I pray for them. I am not praying for the world, but for those you have given me, for they are yours." Jesus consistently and boldly prayed for every aspect of His disciples' lives. What is your next step in moving more toward discipling like Jesus discipled? Be specific:

Fourth, Jesus said, "While I was with them, I protected them and kept them safe by that name you gave me" (v. 12). Jesus clearly protected His disciples by His teaching, His careful observations, and attending to the small details of their lives. What does this look like with your disciples and any next steps you need to take with them?

And then lastly, we have just looked at Jesus' statement, "As you sent me into the world, I have sent them into the world" (v. 18). Jesus was sent, and lived with this realization in every area of His life. What does that mean for you and your disciples? Again, try to be specific:

Reveal the Father . . .
Speak the words given . . .
Pray intentionally . . .
Protect them . . .
Send them out . . .

We can do what Jesus did as we walk as Jesus walked.

Since we are over halfway through this study, reread John 17 and highlight any major new insights that you see in the text.

JESUS PRAYS TO BE GLORIFIED

[1] After Jesus said this, he looked toward heaven and prayed:

"Father, the hour has come. Glorify your Son, that your Son may glorify you. [2] For you granted him authority over all people that he might give eternal life to all those you have given him. [3] Now this is eternal life: that they know you, the only true God, and Jesus Christ, whom you have sent. [4] I have brought you glory on earth by finishing the work you gave me to do. [5] And now, Father, glorify me in your presence with the glory I had with you before the world began.

JESUS PRAYS FOR HIS DISCIPLES

[6] "I have revealed you to those whom you gave me out of the world. They were yours; you gave them to me and they have obeyed your word. [7] Now they know that everything you have given me comes from you. [8] For I gave them the words you gave me and they accepted them. They knew with certainty that I came from you, and they believed that you sent me. [9] I pray for them. I am not praying for the world, but for those you have given me, for they are yours. [10] All I have is yours, and all you have is mine. And glory has come to me through them. [11] I will remain in the world no longer, but they are still in the world, and I am coming to you. Holy Father, protect them by the power of your name, the name you gave me, so that they may be one as we are one. [12] While I was with them, I protected them and kept them safe by that name you gave me. None has been lost except the one doomed to destruction so that Scripture would be fulfilled.

[13] "I am coming to you now, but I say these things while I am still in the world, so that they may have the full measure of my joy within them. [14] I have given them your word and the world has hated them, for they are not of the world any more than I am of the world. [15] My prayer is not that you take them out of the world but that you protect them from the evil one. [16] They are not of the world, even as I am not of it. [17] Sanctify them by the truth; your word is truth. [18] As you sent me into the world, I have sent them into the world. [19] For them I sanctify myself, that they too may be truly sanctified.

JESUS PRAYS FOR ALL BELIEVERS

20 "My prayer is not for them alone. I pray also for those who will believe in me through their message, 21 that all of them may be one, Father, just as you are in me and I am in you. May they also be in us so that the world may believe that you have sent me. 22 I have given them the glory that you gave me, that they may be one as we are one— 23 I in them and you in me—so that they may be brought to complete unity. Then the world will know that you sent me and have loved them even as you have loved me.

24 "Father, I want those you have given me to be with me where I am, and to see my glory, the glory you have given me because you loved me before the creation of the world.

25 "Righteous Father, though the world does not know you, I know you, and they know that you have sent me. 26 I have made you known to them, and will continue to make you known in order that the love you have for me may be in them and that I myself may be in them."

SANCTIFY: "FOR THEM I SANCTIFY MYSELF, THAT THEY TOO MAY BE TRULY SANCTIFIED"

(JOHN 17:19)

Go deeper: Watch videos online and download the Like Jesus app. LikeJesus.church/live

GETTING STARTED

Now we see Jesus making another powerful "I" statement. We see Jesus praying, "For them I sanctify myself, that they too may be truly sanctified" (John 17:19).

How do you currently understand what this means?

It has often been said that you can only reproduce what you are!

And Jesus clearly says, "For them I sanctify myself." Jesus lived a sinless life; the Scriptures tell us on several occasions that He was without sin.

Write out these verses below. (You can often gain new insight as you copy the text and pay close attention to the words.)

2 Corinthians 5:21

Hebrews 4:15

1 Peter 1:18–19

1 Peter 2:22

1 John 3:5

The word "sanctify" (John 17:19) used here is the Greek word that means to "set apart, to cleanse or purify, dedicate, or consecrate."[1] We are told in Hebrews 9:13 that in the Old Testament it was "the blood of goats and bulls and the ashes of a heifer sprinkled on those who are ceremonially unclean *sanctify them* so that they are outwardly clean." Without the shedding of blood there was no forgiveness for sins, for it was the shedding of blood that provided the means for purification.

But now in John 17, Jesus tells us that He has sanctified Himself for their sake. On one level, this final prayer and dedication of Jesus mirrored what the high priest would do before offering a sacrifice. He would offer a final cleansing and dedication to present a pure sacrifice at the hands of a cleansed servant (Lev. 16:4b, 24; Heb. 5:7–10). In a beautiful way, Jesus is dedicating Himself in this final act of prayer before He crosses the Kidron Valley and lays down His life for the sins of the world. This was the ultimate High Priest's dedication to accomplish the ultimate sacrifice. Jesus' entire life was a life of perfect dedication and sinlessness. As Romans 5:10 tells us, the life of Christ saves us because it was a life of perfect obedience all the way to the cross, even death on the cross (Phil. 2:8). But here in John 17, we see Jesus, on one final occasion, dedicating Himself in perfect submission to the final act of atonement for the sins of the world.

Throughout His life, Jesus "sanctified" (set apart) Himself. Every aspect of Jesus' life was an act of obedience and dedication to His Father's will. By entering our world (John 1:14), Jesus obeyed the Father's "sending." As a child, Jesus lived a full and complete life of obedience (Luke 2:51), even when He felt alienated by His brothers and mocked by those in His hometown (Psalm 69:7–12). Jesus obeyed all the way to the cross and even death on a cross (Phil. 2:8). He lived a life of perfect sanctification, dedicating Himself to doing only what pleased His Father. Being the perfect sacrifice, He offered His life by shedding His blood, "a lamb without blemish or defect" (1 Peter 1:19). He became the perfect sacrificial Lamb of God who takes away the sins of the world (John 1:29).

Adam came into a perfect world and chose to sin, but Jesus (the second Adam) came into a sin-soaked world and only chose obedience. As a result He became the perfect Lamb of God who could take away the sin of the world—including yours and mine. Rising from the grave, He ascended into heaven. Seated at the right hand of the Father, He was given a gift: the gift of the promised Holy Spirit (Acts 2:33), which He poured out in our life. "For just as through the disobedience of the one man the many were made sinners, so also through the obedience of the one man the many will be made righteous" (Rom. 5:19). We become like Him as He gives to us (imputes to us) His righteousness. Christ's perfect life of complete sanctification provided the perfect atonement for our sins.

As Jesus predicted in John 12:23–24 (and prayed here in John 17), "The hour has come for the Son of Man to be glorified. Very truly I tell you, unless a kernel of wheat falls to the ground and dies, it remains only a single seed. But if it dies, it produces many seeds." Don't miss the power of this principle!

Let me make this extremely practical. We reproduce who we are! This is a principle that Jesus set up when He created the world. In Genesis 1:11 (21, 24) God made His

> In a beautiful way, Jesus is dedicating Himself in this final act of prayer, before He crosses the Kidron Valley and lays down His life for the sins of the world. This was the ultimate High Priest dedication to accomplish the ultimate sacrifice.

creation and told them to multiply "according to their own kind." He could have set it up differently; fruit trees multiplying wheat plants, cows giving birth to chickens, corn plants yielding a field of barley—but He didn't. You multiply after your own kind!

In the same way, Jesus' life of perfect sanctification multiplied many seeds of righteous children. His perfect life paid for our sins, so that in God's eyes we are as righteous as His Son.

Before we explore the practical nature of this principle, stop and thank the Lord for His life of perfect obedience, which made His atonement complete for us. Write out a simple prayer expressing your gratitude:

DAY ONE

A LIFE OF SANCTIFICATION

The text is clear, Jesus says, "For them I sanctify myself, that they too may be fully sanctified." Jesus lived a pure life set apart, so that we too could live a cleansed and pure life unto Him.

During the next three days, I want to look very practically at what this means, as we learn how the Master Disciple-maker lived out this discipline.

I want us to begin by looking at Jesus when, for the first time, He told His disciples that He "must go to Jerusalem and suffer many things at the hands of the elders, the chief priests and the teachers of the law, and that he must be killed and on the third day be raised to life" (Matthew 16:21–28).

Read this story in Matthew 16:21–28, and underline whatever stands out to you as you read the text:

> ²¹ From that time on Jesus began to explain to his disciples that he must go to Jerusalem and suffer many things at the hands of the elders, the chief priests and the teachers of the law, and that he must be killed and on the third day be raised to life.
>
> ²² Peter took him aside and began to rebuke him. "Never, Lord!" he said. "This shall never happen to you!"
>
> ²³ Jesus turned and said to Peter, "Get behind me, Satan! You are a stumbling block to me; you do not have in mind the concerns of God, but merely human concerns."
>
> ²⁴ Then Jesus said to his disciples, "Whoever wants to be my disciple must deny themselves and take up their cross and follow me. ²⁵ For whoever wants to save their life will lose it, but whoever loses their life for me will find it. ²⁶ What good will it be for someone to gain the whole world, yet forfeit their soul? Or what can anyone give in exchange for their soul? ²⁷ For the Son of Man is going to come in

his Father's glory with his angels, and then he will reward each person according to what they have done.

[28] "Truly I tell you, some who are standing here will not taste death before they see the Son of Man coming in his kingdom."

This event is approximately nine months before Jesus will be put on the cross. Jesus knows it will be this Passover; perhaps His Father revealed this to Him the night after He was informed of John's death and spent nine hours in prayer (Matt. 14:23). We discussed this event in chapter 5. Taking His disciples way up north to Caesarea Philippi, a pagan city where Jews would not usually go, Jesus intentionally asks His disciples who people say He is. After this exchange, where Peter answers correctly, Jesus begins to tell His disciples that He must go to Jerusalem and die. And then He turns the tables and says to His disciples, in the same way, you too must be willing to "take up [your] cross and follow me" (Matt. 16:24).

As I have studied these last nine months of Jesus' ministry, I found six words that powerfully convey Jesus' total willingness to set Himself apart (sanctify Himself) for others' sake.

Let's look at these six words that describe Christ's attitude, since we are called to "think and act like Christ Jesus" (Phil. 2:5 NCV). In Matthew 16 Jesus tells us that in the same way, we must be willing to take up our cross and follow Him. Paul clearly says the same in Philippians 3:10 when he says we are "becom[ing] like him in his death."

WILLINGLY

Read John 10:18 and write it below:

WEEK 8 | SANCTIFY: "FOR THEM I SANCTIFY MYSELF, THAT THEY TOO MAY BE TRULY SANCTIFIED"

What is this verse telling us about the attitude of Jesus as He moved toward the cross?

In the same way, what does this look like in our life as we willingly move toward taking up our cross daily? Be specific:

Describe what it looks like for someone to be unwilling to take up their cross daily.

Stop and pray, asking the Lord to help you be willing in every area of your cross bearing.

INTENTIONALLY

Read Luke 9:51 and rewrite it in your own words:

Describe some of the many times in which Jesus could have escaped from going to Jerusalem to die, even on the very last night in the garden. What are some ways He could have avoided the cross?

What does it mean for us to "resolutely," "stedfastly" (KJV), or "intently set [our] face" (HNV) toward dying to self? Try to be specific:

So often when I see mocking, ridicule, persecution, or suffering in my future, I turn and go the opposite direction. Why do you think Jesus didn't respond this way? Think carefully about this:

DAY TWO

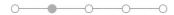

A LIFESTYLE OF DEDICATION

As we continue on the journey with Jesus toward the cross, we too want to live a life of dedication and set ourselves apart like Jesus prayed in John 17:19, "that they too may be truly sanctified." Or as Paul prayed in Philippians 3:10, that we may become "like him in his death."

Yesterday we saw how Jesus willingly and intentionally set His face toward Jerusalem. Today we want to look at two more words that describe what Jesus modeled for us.

LOVINGLY

Read John 3:16 and 1 John 3:16. How are they similar? What is this telling us about how Jesus died on the cross?

What is 1 John 3:16 telling us we ought to do because of what Jesus did for us? Explain what this looks like right now in your world and life situation:

1 Peter 2:21–23 tells us something similar, but accents a couple of different attitudes Jesus displayed as He suffered on the cross. What are those practical attitudes and how do they demonstrate love?

What is the opposite of this verse? In other words, what attitude is the opposite of doing what Jesus did here in 1 Peter 2?

COURAGEOUSLY

Psalm 44:22 is another verse telling us how Jesus approached Jerusalem. Jesus surely knew this verse and clearly knew what He was facing. What does this verse tell us about Jesus' attitude as He entered Jerusalem?

In Romans 8:36, Paul uses this same verse to tell us we have nothing to fear. Look up these verses surrounding Romans 8:36 and write down, in your own words, Paul's conclusions because of Jesus' actions:

Romans 8:31

Romans 8:33

Romans 8:35

Romans 8:37

Stop right now and ask the Lord to help you to approach your daily cross with this same attitude of courage and confidence. Rejoice in what Paul says in the verses above.

DAY THREE

BECOMING LIKE HIM
IN HIS DEATH

As Jesus continues to move toward Jerusalem during His last six months, you find Him on at least two different occasions telling His disciples what awaits Him (Matt. 16:21; Mark 10:32–34). He knew clearly what was ahead of Him, yet continued on His journey. Mark tells us that as Jesus led the way, His disciples "were astonished, while those who followed were afraid" (Mark 10:32). Because of this response, the crowds also knew trouble and conflict lay ahead.

ENTRUSTED

How could Jesus continue this way? Read what the end of the verse in 1 Peter 2:23 tells us and write it below in your own words: what was Jesus' attitude?

Luke 23:46 gives us this same perspective, but stated in a different way. What does Jesus' statement in this verse communicate? Write it in your own words:

Faith is the opposite of sin. When we sin, we are trusting our own abilities and our own assessment of what is right and wrong. When we live by faith, we are trusting God. Jesus lived a perfect life of complete faith. The Scripture is so clear about the importance of living by faith. Read these verses and write them out in your own words:

Romans 14:23b

Galatians 3:11

Hebrews 11:6

1 John 5:4

As we face our daily cross, how does an attitude of faith conquer the consequences of this fallen world and the suffering that we will surely face? What does this practically look like in your life today? Be specific:

THE RIGHT FOCUS

So far we have seen how Jesus willingly, intentionally, lovingly, and courageously entrusted Himself to the Father as He made His way to Jerusalem to die on the cross. In that same way, we too are to become "like him in his death" (Phil. 3:10) and "take up [our] cross daily" (Luke 9:23).

But another word captures what Jesus models for us—one that we so often want to ignore.

ENDURED

What does Hebrews 12:2 tell us about how Jesus approached the cross? Write it out in your own words:

Endurance is difficult! So often in the Christian life, the endurance we are called to exhibit comes with ridicule and even mocking or "shame"—to use the word here in Hebrews 12:2. And because of this "shame," endurance becomes even more demanding.

"Despising (scorning) the shame" (ESV) seems almost impossible when we face it in our lives. How did Jesus so willingly, intentionally, lovingly, and courageously endure the cross while entrusting Himself to His Father? Could there be more to this life lesson than what we are presently seeing? Does Jesus model something more for us by what He prayed in John 17:19 when He said He sanctified (dedicated) Himself?

Going back to these last nine months in Jesus' life, when He sets His face toward Jerusalem and so powerfully dedicates (sanctifies) Himself to that which the Father had called Him, I think we can also learn another critical lesson from His example.

Do you see in Hebrews 12:2 the reason why Jesus was able to endure? Write that reason below:

After Jesus told His disciples that He must go to Jerusalem and die, He takes James, Peter, and John up to the mountain where He is transfigured before them. Moses and Elijah appear. What does Luke 9:31 say that Jesus spoke to them about?

Do you suppose the heavenly Father meant to encourage Jesus by sending Elijah and Moses to speak to Jesus? More than ten times in the next few months Jesus states that His focus is beyond the cross.

Read Luke 9:51. What does it say was near? (Notice it does not say His suffering.)

Read John 7:33. How much longer was Jesus with them and where is He headed?

Read John 8:14. What did Jesus know?

Read John 12:23. What time was it? (Notice what Jesus does not say.)

Read John 13:1. What did Jesus know, and where was He headed?

Read John 13:33a. What was Jesus thinking about?

Look closely. Jesus did not say here in John 12:23 that it was time for Him to suffer, be mocked, and spit upon and then die. His focus was not on the cross; it was beyond the cross. He was not enduring to just get to the finish line—He was enduring for what was beyond the finish line!

In the same way, what is the principle about endurance that we must learn from Jesus? What must be our focus: the cross or what is beyond our cross? What principles did Paul state so well in 2 Corinthians 4:16–18?

What are the struggles (crosses) that God has asked you to carry in your life? Identify some present concerns that the Lord has asked you to "take up . . . daily and follow me" (Luke 9:23).

Stop right now and think about your attitude toward the cross you carry. Is it like Jesus'? Ask the Lord to help you have "the same mindset" (Phil. 2:5) that He had. Write out a simple prayer asking God to give you His attitude:

Acronyms help me remember important truths. I remember what it means to become "like him in his death" (Phil 3:10) by the acronym WILCEE (willingly, intentionally, lovingly, courageously, entrusted, endured). 1 John 3:2 tells me that "when Christ appears, we shall be like him, for we shall see [WILCEE] him as he is."

John 17:1–2 clearly shows us that Jesus' personal focus was on that which was beyond the cross. His focus was heavenly. Because of this He could endure what He faced in this world. "For them I sanctify myself," Jesus said, "that they too may be truly sanctified" (John 17:19).

If our disciples see in us this attitude of Jesus, we too will help them become like Him. Stop and ask the Lord to help you become more like Him today.

SHARE: "I HAVE GIVEN THEM THE GLORY THAT YOU GAVE ME"

(JOHN 17:22)

Go deeper: Watch videos online and download the Like Jesus app. LikeJesus.church/live

GETTING STARTED

Jesus' future glory was a major theme during the last few days of His life on earth. He spoke about it over and over again. Over three hundred times the "glory" of the Lord is referenced in the Scriptures. Matthew and Mark each reference this theme three times, and Luke refers to Jesus' or God's glory six times. But in the gospel of John, "glory" is mentioned over twenty times. And most of those references are by Jesus Himself, especially here in John 17 where He is talking with His Father in heaven.

Read each of these verses in John 17. What can we learn about Jesus' glory from these verses?

Verse 1

Verse 4

Verse 5

Verse 10

Verse 22

Over three
hundred times
the "glory" of
the Lord is
referenced in
the Scriptures.

Verse 24

In verse 22, the verse we want to look at this week, what is your initial impression of
what it means when Jesus said, "I have given them the glory that you gave me"?

DAY ONE

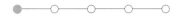

MAN'S SHADED AND BROKEN GLORY

When Jesus says, "I have given them the glory that you gave me"—what did that mean? It is an amazing statement! While it may mean many things, this week I'd like to explain my understanding of this incredible statement.

In verse 2 of John 17, Jesus in His prayer makes an interesting connection with the dual phrase of "glorify your Son, that your Son may glorify you" (verse 1). He then says, "since you have given him authority over all flesh, to give eternal life to all whom you have given him" (verse 2, ESV). His glory is seemingly linked to the authority Jesus has been given.

We know that Jesus came from glory and was returning to glory, but here in John 17 Jesus is seemingly speaking of a new and greater glory. John 7:39 says that "for as yet the Spirit had not been given, because Jesus was not yet glorified" (ESV).

Hebrews 2:9b gives us some more insight saying, "namely Jesus, crowned with glory and honor because of the suffering of death" (ESV). The whole theme of Hebrews 2 is that of Jesus' humanity. He had to become fully human, like us in every way yet without sin, for our atonement to become complete (Heb. 2:17). Or as it says here in verse 9, He had to "taste death for everyone."

But something very powerful and very profound happened when Jesus became the sacrificial Lamb of God to take away our sins. Let's look closer at Hebrews to appreciate what Jesus did for us.

Hebrews 1 tells us that Jesus was "appointed the heir of all things" and that He was "the exact imprint of [God's] nature" (vv. 2–3 ESV). But the chapter goes on to say that Jesus was far greater than the angels because "to which of the angels did God ever say, 'You are my Son, today I have begotten you'?" (v. 5 ESV).

But then Hebrews says something amazing. "It is not to angels that he has subjected the world to come" (2:5), and then in verse 16, "it is not angels he helps." The author of Hebrews then turns his attention to mankind, saying:

> "What is man, that you are mindful of him, or the son of man, that you care for him? You made him for a little while lower than the angels; you have crowned him with glory and honor, putting everything in subjection under his feet." Now in putting everything in subjection to him, he left nothing outside his control. At present, we do not yet see everything in subjection to him. But we see him who for a little while was made lower than the angels, namely Jesus . . . (Hebrews 2:6–9 ESV)

Notice carefully what is happening here. The writer of Hebrews is saying that all of God's creation is under (subject to) mankind. That is part of man's original glory and honor. But at present, we no longer see man with all of creation under his dominion. But we do see Jesus, who has total dominion over creation: walking on water, stilling the storm, healing the sick, etc.

Man has fallen. No longer having dominion over creation (Gen. 1:28), man is now lower than the angels, having become a slave of sin and Satan. Jesus entered our world and descended to where we were (yet without sin), to restore God's original creative order: lifting man back to his rightful position as ruler over His creation.

Let me quickly show you one more powerful and profound truth. Turn with me to Psalm 8, from which this Hebrews 2 passage was quoted. I want you to see a major truth in Psalm 8.

Carefully read Psalm 8:5–6 from a good translation. Write it below to help you grasp every word of it:

Jesus entered our world and descended to where we were (yet without sin), to restore God's original creative order: lifting man back to his rightful position as ruler over His creation.

How does it differ from the Hebrews 2 quote?

Psalm 8:5 tells us that man is made "a little lower than the heavenly beings" (ESV). Here the word "heavenly beings" is the word *elohim*, which is used over 2,600 times in the Scriptures and most every time translated "God." Here it is translated as "heavenly beings."

Do you see the truth? In God's original created order, man was made in the image of God and just a little lower than Elohim (first column in diagram below). Since angels were created before man, many speculate that Lucifer (Satan) did not like the fact that he no longer would be the most magnificent of God's creation, so he tempted Adam and Eve to sin and made them his slaves. Satan now controlled fallen man through his sinful nature and was given control of this broken fallen world (Matt. 4:8–9) (second column below under Genesis 3). God's intended order for creation was broken, and Jesus came to restore man back to God's intended position as a little lower than Elohim. He was to have dominion over creation as Psalm 8:6 and Hebrews 2:8 says (last column below).

Below is a diagram of that reality.

Genesis 1–2, Psalm 8:5–6	Genesis 3	After resurrection (Heb. 2)
God	God	God
Man	Angels (Satan)	Man
Angels	Man (slave)	Angels

DAY TWO

CHRIST'S ULTIMATE GLORY

When Christ returned to heaven, not only did He return to His former glory but, as John 17 tells us, He returns to a greater glory. He now has all authority under Him with all of those whom He has redeemed. His kingdom was launched. Man was restored to his former position, now having been "raised . . . up with Christ and seated us with him in the heavenly realms in Christ Jesus" (Eph. 2:6).

Christ's greater glory is now fully as "Lord of lords and King of kings" (Rev. 17:14). As head of His church, He will one day return, having all judgment placed under Him.

What does Revelation 5:9–10 tell us about the present glory of Christ?

What additional thought does Revelation 5:12–13 and 7:9–10 add?

While in His humanity, Jesus makes some amazing statements. What does John 13:3 say about Jesus' authority? (See also Luke 10:22a.)

In John 17:2 Jesus links His being glorified with the reality that His Father had given Him authority over all flesh. Would you conclude that His glorification directly relates to His now being the King of this new and coming kingdom? Why or why not? Explain your answer.

DAY THREE

THE GLORY JESUS SHARES WITH US

Yesterday we realized that Jesus' new and greater glory involved, in part, His having all authority in heaven and on earth placed under His kingship. Having restored fallen man to his intended position in God's created order, Jesus now returns to heaven to the fullness of that greater glory.

With this perspective of Jesus' glory, what does this tell us about the glory that Christ has shared with us? What do you think that glory is?

Read Revelation 5:9–10. What does this passage tell us about our future role in the restored creative order? What does that look like to you? Try to be specific.

What does 2 Timothy 2:11–13 tell us?

How does 1 Peter 2:9 describe us?

Theologians often speak of the "now and not yet" kingdom of Christ. The "now" aspect of the kingdom is the spiritual rule and reign of Christ over His bride, the church. We have been restored to our rightful position as "just a little lower than Elohim." We have been made a "chosen people, a royal priesthood, a holy nation, God's special possession" (1 Peter 2:9). We shall rule and reign with Him now in that spiritual kingdom which continues to grow and expand. Wow—what shared glory Jesus so freely gives to us!

But I'm also of the persuasion that one day there will be a literal rule and reign of Christ on this earth. This is the "not yet" aspect of the kingdom rule and reign of Christ. During that literal 1,000-year reign (the millennium), Christ will literally reign as the true Son of David on this earth (Rev. 20). While I know there are many views on the millennium and anything related to future events, let me briefly give you my under-standing, which so powerfully captures what Jesus gave to us in John 17:22.

I like to think in terms of 5 Rs as I lay out this future.

RETURN: Revelation 22:12a makes it clear, "Look, I am coming soon!" With dozens of verses on the first coming of Christ, and all of them literally fulfilled, we have even more verses on Christ's second coming.

REWARD: Revelation 22:12b, "My reward is with me." What is that reward? I believe it is the privilege of ruling and reigning with Him. As He returns to His chosen city (2 Chron. 6:6) in Jerusalem, from there we will go out to rule and reign with Him (Rev. 19:14; Zech. 14:9).

RESTORE: The Scripture tells us in Acts 3:21, "Heaven must receive him until the time comes for God to restore everything, as he promised long ago through his holy proph-ets." The word here for "restore" means the restoration to a former state. I believe God will use us to bring about that restoration. While He could do it instantly, from my per-spective it would be just like God to use us to restore the earth to its former glory. Our reward could then be the incredible privilege of restoring this world to its former glory, alongside of all the saints through the generations. This will give us the privilege to do what Adam and Eve should have done in the garden. We are told in Matthew 25:21 that to the degree in which we have been faithful is the degree to which we will rule and reign with Him and enter into the "master's happiness." Wow!

RENEW: In Matthew 19:27–28, Peter asks Jesus, What will be there for us when all these things come to pass? Jesus clearly states, "Truly I tell you, at the renewal of all things, when the Son of Man sits on his glorious throne, you who have followed me will also sit on twelve thrones, judging the twelve tribes of Israel." He then goes on to say that this reward will be one hundred times greater than what we gave up. The word here for "renewal" is the Greek word *palingenesia*, meaning "new birth" or "regeneration." It is only used one other time in the New Testament in Titus 3:5. There it refers to the Christian's new birth.

I believe this will happen when Christ returns, Satan is bound in the abyss (Rev. 20:2) and the curse is lifted (Rom. 8:19–21). Imagine a world in which Satan is bound, the curse has been lifted, and our sinful body is now a glorified body. In this world where Satan is bound, when we go out to fix something, it will stay fixed. No more decay, no more brokenness, no more sin. Working together with Him and believers through the ages, we will rule and reign, renewing the world to its former glory. While we are doing this, we will be spending countless hours of sharing stories of His marvelous grace as we tell each other our stories. We will mingle with David and Paul, Peter and Andrew, Mary and Sarah, and thousands of other believers through the ages, praising Him who redeemed us. What a wonderful reward under the unified rule of the King of kings and Lord of lords.

REVEAL: As Romans 8:18–19 says, all creation longs for God's glory to be revealed in us and in His creation. As we restore the earth to its former pre-fallen state, we will daily worship Him as we reveal, see, and learn more and more of His glorious creation. Trees and flowers and lakes are beautiful now—imagine them when Satan is bound and the curse is lifted. A new and magnificent beauty, reflecting the beauty of our God's creative genius. In the process, we will worship Him over and over, with ever-increasing awe as we see His magnificent beauty revealed in creation.

What in this picture of the future captures your imagination for what it will be like one day? How does your picture differ?

DAY FOUR

BECOMING MORE LIKE JESUS IN OUR DISCIPLING

This week we have tried to capture what Jesus meant when He said, "I have given them the glory that you gave me." Jesus genuinely shared His glory with His disciples. And He also shares that with us since He also prays for us (John 17:20), and because we are the disciples of these disciples.

What do you think it looks like when we (like Jesus) share glory with our disciples? Be as practical as you can be.

What does it look like when we do not share glory with our disciples? Can you give any personal examples of this?

How can we live out this principle of sharing the glory with new believers? Think about those you listed in chapter 2:

What does this (sharing of glory) look like with more mature believers who are engaged in the work of the ministry with you?

What could this look like with non-Christians, who are still created in the image of God, but yet to be redeemed?

Describe someone you know who is really good at sharing the glory with others.

—

MISSIONAL: "FISHERS OF MEN"

(MATTHEW 4:19c ESV)

Go deeper: Watch videos online and download the Like Jesus app. LikeJesus.church/live

GETTING STARTED

In order to define disciple-making according to Jesus' own words, we have used Jesus' challenge to His initial ministry team in Matthew 4:19 where He said, "Follow me, and I will make you fishers of men" (ESV).

So we began this study by stating that discipling Jesus-style is relational ("follow me"), intentional ("I will make you") and now missional ("fishers of men"). Under *intentional* we looked at Jesus' prayer in John 17, and from His own words we looked at seven priorities Jesus Himself mentioned: reveal, speak, pray, protect, send, sanctify, and share.

Let's now turn our attention to missional. In week 2, we discussed how focused Jesus was in teaching His disciples to reproduce. In one sense, we have never made a fully trained disciple until our disciples reproduce. A fully trained disciple is someone who multiplies both the character and priorities of Jesus into others' lives. This was the passion and focus of Jesus' whole ministry: reproduction. Making disciples who could make disciples.

Biblically and organically, "fruit" has always been a picture of reproduction. In John 15, Jesus explained to His disciples, just before He prays for them in John 17, about four levels of fruit bearing: no fruit (John 15:2a), fruit (15:2b), more fruit (15:2c), and much fruit (15:8). In this last verse, Jesus makes a powerful statement when He says, "By this my Father is glorified, that you bear *much fruit* and so prove to be my disciples" (ESV). God's agenda for all of us is to bear much fruit! This is a process that takes time.

Farmers naturally understand the principle of multiplication from the illustration of fruit. Growing up on a farm in South Dakota, my Dad did everything he could to multiply the fruit of his harvest. Farmers also know that you can't make fruit happen. Fruit is a by-product of doing certain things well. You cultivate the soil, plant the seeds, fertilize the soil, remove the weeds, and pray continually. Fruit is a by-product.

My dad spent years studying how to produce more fruit. Growing a lot of corn, the average yield was around 120 bushels per acre. Some years we would get a "bumper crop" of 180 bushels; and in some years, when there was little rain or the sun too hot, we only got 50 bushels per acre. In the "dirty '30s" the average yield was less than 10 bushels per acre.

A fully trained disciple is someone who multiplies both the character and priorities of Jesus into others' lives.

But my dad tenaciously studied and measured the yearly yield of fruit. Planting rows and rows of different types of seeds, planted at different times of the year, and with different types of fertilizer, my father mastered the "fruit production," often outproducing every other farmer in the region. Why? Because he mastered the basics. Knowing that fruit was a by-product of doing the right things, at the right time, in the right way, he increased the yearly production of that fruit.

In the same way, spiritual fruit doesn't "just happen." It is a by-product of daily disciplines done well. Fruit biblically involves three things: character (fruit of the Spirit; Gal. 5:22–23), conduct (acts of service; Col. 1:10), and converts (Rom. 1:13).

My first study, *Walk Like Jesus*, examines what it means to live out 1 John 2:6, to walk as Jesus walked. That study looks at six major priorities Jesus modeled: Holy Spirit dependence, Prayerful guidance, Obedience learned, Word centered, Exalting His Father, and Relationships of love and integrity. HS POWER became our acronym to understand how Jesus walked in His humanity.

Here in this study, *Live Like Jesus*, we've begun to look at Christ's disciplines. While in no way is this comprehensive, we have focused upon His prayer in John 17 and His statement in Matthew 4:19.

In the cover of my Bible, about thirty years ago, I wrote out my life's mission statement. It was simply what I have sensed is God's calling on my life. It reads, "Out of the overflow of my love for God, to multiply the character and priorities of Jesus in as many people as possible." When I first wrote this personal mission statement, I soon learned this was impossible for me to do. I could not make it happen. But I could focus on certain disciplines that produce this fruit. And that has been my life focus.

Jesus' whole agenda was to create a movement of multiplying disciples—making disciples who could make disciples. Fruit was His end product. In John 17, we have seen seven intentional disciplines (methods) of Jesus, as He expressed in His prayer for His disciples. In the same way, we cannot make a disciple who makes a disciple. But we can focus on those disciplines that increase the odds of producing disciple-makers. Let me summarize those intentional disciplines:

1. REVEAL: Doing everything we can to reveal the Father to those God brings into our lives through teaching, modeling, exhorting, and prayer.

2. SPEAK: Listening well as we study God's Word, with an ear to hearing what the Spirit wants to say to us and then speaking to those God has brought into our lives.

3. PRAY: Intentionally prioritizing those God has put around us, and lifting them up in weekly prayer.

4. PROTECT: Carefully observing and then exhorting our disciples in an effort to protect them from the evil one.

5. SEND: Personally living a "sent missional lifestyle" and then helping our disciples to do the same.

6. SANCTIFY: Consecrating our own life to provide a shield of protection for our disciples, knowing that we reproduce who we are.

7. SHARE: Building up and sharing with our disciples any honor that comes our way, teaching and encouraging them to keep their eyes on the future glory that we will one day fully experience.

> Jesus' whole agenda was to create a movement of multiplying disciples—making disciples who could make disciples. Fruit was His end product.

As you think about the present fruit of your life, how does the fruit that you yield reflect the disciplines you live out?

Are you satisfied with the present "fruit" of your life? Why or why not?

Which of the seven disciplines that Jesus mentioned in John 17 are you most effective at?

Which discipline needs more focused attention? Why and how can this improve?

DAY ONE

DISCIPLING PRE-CHRISTIANS

My simple definition of a disciple is someone who "follows Christ, and seeks to fully reflect both His character and priorities." His character is reflected in the fruit of the Spirit. His priorities are reflected in reproducing other disciple-makers.

Thus, my definition of discipling is simply to "help people to follow Christ, fully living out His character and priorities."

We have mentioned already that making disciples is different than "discipleship." Discipleship means to help people to grow spiritually, whereas "mak[ing] disciples" (Matt. 28:16–20) involves the whole process of winning the lost, building up new believers, and then equipping workers to repeat the process.

With this perspective, I want to turn our attention now to practically living out what you have just studied. Non-Christians—or, as I like to call them, pre-Christians—are not yet following Jesus. Therefore, discipling pre-Christians means helping them get to the place where they are willing to repent of their sin, turn from that sin, and believe on Jesus as their Savior and Lord. Helping pre-Christians get to this place is a process I like to describe as Spiritual CPR.

> Discipling pre-Christians means helping them get to the place where they are willing to repent of their sin, turn from that sin, and believe on Jesus as their Savior and Lord.

Physical CPR is when we resuscitate a life. Spiritual CPR is when we help people receive the new life of Christ. Isaiah 28:23–27 describes this CPR process as Cultivating (breaking up the hardened ground, or becoming "a friend of sinners"), Planting (sowing seeds in different ways at different times) and then Reaping (clearly and concisely sharing the gospel to reap the harvest). Spiritual CPR: discipling the lost person toward a willingness to begin to follow Jesus.

With this in mind, list three pre-Christians the Lord has placed in your life that you want to disciple. You may want to list one at the Cultivating level (building a friendship with), one at the Planting level (beginning to share God's truth with), and then one at the Reaping level (ready to hear the gospel clearly and concisely). On the left hand side, I have listed the seven disciplines that Jesus mentioned about how He discipled. Looking at this chart, write down your next steps for each person.

Pre-Christians			
Names:	#1	#2	#3
What Jesus did:	What we can do as a next step:		
Reveal: Model and teach			
Speak: Listen and give			
Pray: Intentional and specific			
Protect: Watch and instruct			
Send: Engage and model			
Sanctify: Dedicate and live pure			
Share: Teach and honor			

DAY TWO

DISCIPLING NEW BELIEVERS

How sad it is when people give birth to a baby, only to abandon that baby in an orphanage. And yet how often does this happen in our churches—spiritual babies floundering because they have no spiritual parents to nurture and teach them.

New Christians need five basic skills to mature to the adolescent stage. They need to learn whose they are, their "identity" in Christ. They need to learn how to "feed" themselves, first being fed and then slowly trained to digest God's Word on their own. They need to learn how to "walk," first being carried and then slowly taught to take steps of walking as Jesus walked. They need to learn to "talk," sharing their story and then ultimately God's story. And then finally they need to "clean" themselves, taking cleansing baths and then finally learning to live the cleansed life. (These five basic skills are defined in my book *4 Chair Discipling* in greater detail.)

Discipling new believers is a fun but demanding task. It is extremely critical for future growth and multiplication. So many do nothing intentionally with new believers, because they keep waiting for that perfect curriculum and perfect process. There is none. The best bet is to just get started with whatever resources you have. And the Bible is really all you need. Study John or Colossians or Romans. Begin and allow the relationship to develop.

On the following page, write the names of two new or younger Christians that you know need to be discipled. Using the chart from the John 17 prayer of Jesus, write down your next steps.

New Christians need five basic skills to mature to the adolescent stage.

Young Christians		
Names:	#1	#2
What Jesus did:	What we can do as a next step:	
Reveal: Model and teach		
Speak: Listen and give		
Pray: Intentional and specific		
Protect: Watch and instruct		
Send: Engage and model		
Sanctify: Dedicate and live pure		
Share: Teach and honor		

DAY THREE

DISCIPLING COMMITTED WORKERS

When Jesus went to James, John, Andrew, and Peter and said, "Follow me, and I will make you fishers of men" (ESV), he began a two-year journey of pouring into their lives on a deeper level—helping them to become fishers of men and multiplying their lives into others. These individuals had already been with Jesus for a while. They had seen His life and experienced a few of His miracles (John 2). But now Jesus was calling them into a deeper level of accountability and life shaping. Over the next two years you see Jesus with them over forty-six times, but with the crowds only seventeen times. They became His priority, even as He ministered to the crowds. They became His team that was going to multiply into others after He left them. Coleman calls this the "genius of Christ's strategy.[1] Invest in the few, so that ultimately the few could invest in others.

> Invest in the few, so that ultimately the few could invest in others.

They were AFT'R more as seen in Luke 5:1–11 (Available, Faithful, Teachable, and Responding to His leadership). They were some of His best; and He now focused on keeping the healthy, healthy. They became His priority. In the truest sense of the word, these were His committed disciples.

Who are these people in your life? You identified some of these people in chapter 2. Would the list stay the same? You want to get these people right, because they will become your most effective fruit as they multiply into the lives of others. They may not be the sharpest, or the wealthiest, or even the most talented, but they want more and have a heart for God. And for whatever reason, God has put them into your life.

You may not feel that you know what to do with them or may not even feel qualified. But step out in faith and begin to prioritize these few that God has put on your heart. Make them your priority. Pray for them regularly. Ask them how they are doing. Share with them what God is teaching you. Allow God to use you in their life.

On the following page, write the name of one of these people, and from John 17, look at Jesus' priorities and think about what your next step is with this committed worker, to disciple as Jesus discipled.

Committed Worker	
Name:	#1
What Jesus did:	What we can do as a next step:
Reveal: Model and teach	
Speak: Listen and give	
Pray: Intentional and specific	
Protect: Watch and instruct	
Send: Engage and model	
Sanctify: Dedicate and live pure	
Share: Teach and honor	

Take these six people that you have identified (three pre-Christians, two new or growing believers, and one committed worker), and transfer their names to the sheet on the back of this study. We call this your Circle of Concern. Place it in your Bible or on your desk. Use it as a reminder to make them a priority.

Your Circles

Circles are the people God has placed around you that you are committing to pray for and engage with at their spiritual level. **Identify a few names for each circle and write them below.**

UNBELIEVERS

Those that don't know Jesus.

(at least 3 people)

NEWER BELIEVERS

Those you are actively discipling to go deeper in their walk with Jesus.

(at least 2 people)

ACCOUNTABILITY

A like-minded disciple-maker for encouragement

(at least 1 person)

YOU CAN DO THIS!

Let me remind you of some of Jesus' last words to us in the Great Commission of Matthew 28 (my paraphrase): *Because all authority in heaven and on earth has been given to me, I want you, as you go through your everyday life, to prioritize making disciples like I did. Become a friend of sinners, put Me into that friendship, baptizing those that repent and believe in Me, and then teach them to repeat this process with others. That is my commission to you. And it is the greatest of all causes! And I will be with you every moment until the end to help you do this. Keep your eyes on Me and allow Me to work through you.*

Don't make this harder than it is. Imagine ten years from now, if each year you prioritize a few and teach them to do the same. For illustration sake, imagine with me if every three years, like Jesus, you would just multiply this lifestyle into three others, teaching them to do the same. At the end of ten years there would be over one hundred of you. At the end of twenty years, there would be over one thousand of you. In John 14:12 Jesus said, "Very truly I tell you, whoever believes in me will do the works I have been doing, and they will do even greater things than these, because I am going to the Father." Wouldn't it be great twenty years from now to have multiplied your life in over one thousand disciple-makers?

Jesus in four years made twelve committed disciples and left behind 120 believers (Acts 1:15). And He told us to do what He did, walking as He walked.

Let me tell you about Mark. Mark was in my youth group and at fourteen God got ahold of his life. He learned discipling and now leads our ministry in Latin America. Each year He identifies at least four young men to pour into, and now twenty years later He has thousands of disciples throughout Latin America and beyond.

Let me tell you about Dave. Dave spent an evening in our home and God bonded our hearts. He was beginning a youth ministry training in Eastern Europe, and I shared with him what I was learning about discipling from the life of Christ. Now Dave has over three hundred staff in Eastern Europe and each year tens of thousands hear the gospel and they have thousands of disciples throughout Europe. Simply walking as Jesus walked.

I could go on.

When I was a simple farm boy from South Dakota, a professor at Bible school chal-lenged me to study the life of Christ and do what Jesus did. We called our youth group Sonlife since we were just trying to live out the Son's life, doing what Jesus did. Now, forty years later, it has multiplied into 137 countries (as of this last year). And, not because of me! We are simply seeking to do what Jesus did, the way Jesus did it, and multiplication has been the by-product.

Don't delay. Begin now. Ask Him for the supernatural. In the upper room, Jesus said on six different occasions, "Ask"! In John 16:24, just prior to His prayer in John 17, Jesus said: "Until now you have not asked for anything in my name. Ask and you will receive, and your joy will be complete."

Through Christ, you can do this!

What are you going to ask God for?

Who can you take through this study to begin the process with?

ACKNOWLEDGMENTS

Live Like Jesus is the result of many lessons my coworkers have helped me to learn through the years. While I have developed the core of this study, many have contributed in various ways. My deep respect and appreciation go to:

- The Leadership Team of Global Youth Initiative: John Abrahamse, Florence Fokoua, and M'Gliwe Simdinatome in Africa; Mark Edwards, Michele Montenegro, and Araya Diego in Latin America; Bill Hodgson in Australia; Dave Patty and Maruska Skonc in Eastern Europe; Andrew Tay and Tat Him Chin in Singapore; Benjamin Francis in India; along with Steve Hudson and Don Roscoe in North America. Your tireless efforts to see movements of multiplying disciples in your region of the world has been a great inspiration.

- The New Leadership Team of Sonlife Ministries: Doug Holiday, Josh Yates, Joel Zaborowski, Calvin Russel, and Dean Plumlee. Thanks for providing leadership for the next generation of youth leaders in North America.

- The faithful prayer supporters and donors of GYI, who keep us out on the front lines of ministry by your sacrificial gifts.

- The hundreds of Sonlife certified trainers and 2:6 Group Facilitators who through the years have sacrificially invested in teaching the life of Christ to that next generation. "As iron sharpens iron" (Prov. 27:17), we continue to learn from each other new aspects of Christ's life. I can't think of anyone I'd rather go off to battle with.

- To Dennis Moore for working so hard to put together the Leader's Guide to help us all be more effective in leading others in this study.

- To Randall Payleitner for his constant encouragement in putting this study together, and the rest of the Moody Publishers team who were a joy to work with throughout this process.

NOTES

WEEK 1

1. Robert E. Coleman, *The Master Plan of Evangelism* (Grand Rapids: Revell, 1963; repr. 1993), 33.

WEEK 2

1. John 1:39 records that it was the tenth hour, which was 4 p.m. on the Jewish clock. The next day would begin at sunset in the Jewish calendar, about 6 p.m., meaning at the minimum Jesus spent two hours with them.

WEEKS 3–9 JOHN 17

1. Philip Melanchthon, quoted in Kent Hughes, *John: That You May Believe* (Wheaton, IL: Crossway Books, 1999), 391.

2. Merrill C. Tenney, *John: The Gospel of Belief* (Grand Rapids: Eerdmans, 1948), 243.

3. Ibid., 244.

4 Hughes, *John: That You May Believe*, 391.

WEEK 3

1. Author's paraphrase; *diatribō*, Blue Letter Bible, https://www.blueletterbible.org/lang/lexicon/lexicon.cfm?t=kjv&strongs=g1304.

2. Robert Emerson Coleman, Timothy K. Beougher, Tom Phillips, and William A. Shell, *Disciple Making: Training Leaders to Make Disciples: A Self-Study Course in Understanding and Applying Jesus' Command to "Make Disciples"* (Wheaton, IL: Institute of Evangelism, 1994), 19.

3. Author's paraphrase; *asynetos*, Blue Letter Bible, https://www.blueletterbible.org/lang/lexicon/lexicon.cfm?Strongs=G801.

WEEK 4

1. W. E. Vine, Entry for 'Word,' in *Vine's Expository Dictionary of NT Words* (1940), StudyLight.org, https://www.studylight.org/dictionaries/ved/w/word.html.

WEEK 6

1. *33 Things That Happen at Salvation* is a booklet that can be purchased from Sonlife Ministries at Sonlife.com/resources. It contains a biblical list of thirty-three things that happen at the moment of salvation. It is a simple study that can be worked through easily.

WEEK 7

1. Howard A. Snyder, *Liberating the Church : The Ecology of Church and Kingdom* (Eugene, OR: Wipf and Stock, 1996), 11.

2. I have written a more extensive paper on the pattern of Jesus in regards to suffering titled "The Pattern of Jesus in Regards to Suffering." This has been used around the globe for group discussion. You can download a free copy of this article at gyi.cc/gyi-papers/philosophy-of-ministry/

WEEK 8

1. Author's paraphrase; *hagiazō*, Blue Letter Bible, https://www.blueletterbible.org/lang/lexicon/lexicon.cfm?Strongs=G37.

WEEK 10

1. Robert E. Coleman, *The Master Plan of Evangelism* (Grand Rapids: Revell, 1963; repr. 1993), 33.

ABOUT THE AUTHOR

Dr. Dann Spader is currently serving as founder of Global Youth Initiative. For twenty-five years, Dann served as director of Sonlife Ministries. He has also served for twelve years in a pastoral role in churches. Dann is the father of three daughters, Julie, Jamie, and Christy. He lives in Peoria, Arizona, with his wife Char.

Dann graduated from Moody Bible Institute in 1975 with a BA in Evangelism. He received both a MRE and DMin from Trinity Evangelical Divinity School in Deerfield, Illinois, and has also done graduate work at Wheaton College.

Dann has written over twenty leadership training manuals, contributed several chapters in books, written numerous articles, and produced multiple training videos. Over 750,000 leaders in North America have been through face-to-face training with material Dann has written on the life of Christ.

Sonlife Ministries develops disciple-making leadership in local churches across North America. It is committed to training youth leaders in priorities of Great Commission and Great Commandment health as understood in the life of Christ. Dann began Sonlife Ministries in 1979 and now serves as founder. Doug Holiday currently serves as Sonlife's executive director.

Global Youth Initiative (GYI) is an alliance of more than eighty ministries around the globe, which are committed to creating indigenous movements of multiplication with younger leaders. All of these international ministries are involved in advancing the training and values of the Son's life—many of them having grown out of Sonlife Ministries in North America. These international ministries are in such diverse areas as Africa, Eastern Europe, Central and South America, India, China, Australia, the Middle East, and the Pacific Rim. The vision of GYI is to raise up 100,000 proven young leaders globally, multiplying from everywhere to everywhere.

Dann has recently authored two other resources that focus on the life of Christ. *Walk Like Jesus* is a biblical study that focuses on six character qualities modeled by Jesus. *4 Chair Discipling*, his most recent book, explores how Jesus developed His disciples through four stages of growth and development, teaching them to make disciples who could make disciples.

Your Circles

Circles are the people God has placed around you that you are committing to pray for and engage with at their spiritual level. **Identify a few names for each circle and write them below.**

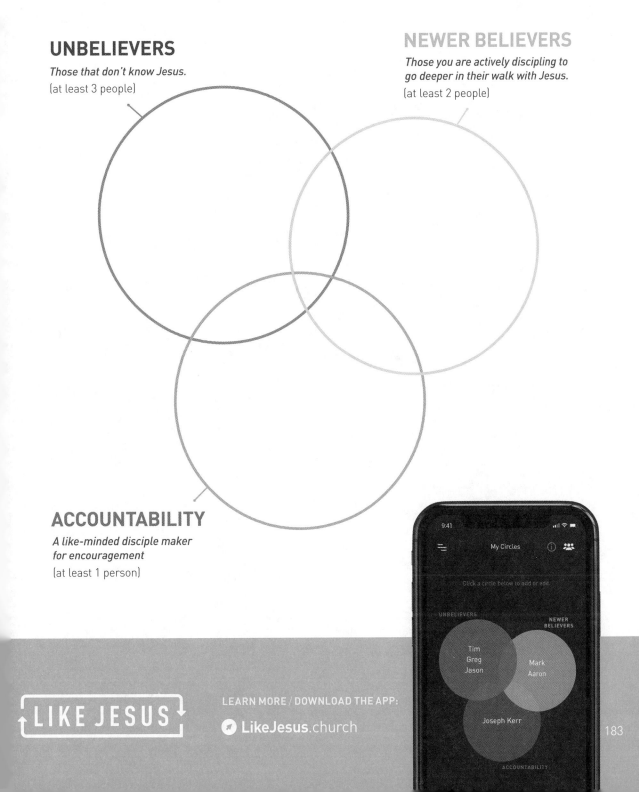

UNBELIEVERS

Those that don't know Jesus.

(at least 3 people)

NEWER BELIEVERS

Those you are actively discipling to go deeper in their walk with Jesus.

(at least 2 people)

ACCOUNTABILITY

A like-minded disciple maker for encouragement

(at least 1 person)

LIKE JESUS

LEARN MORE / DOWNLOAD THE APP:

LikeJesus.church

Your Circles

Circles are the people God has placed around you that you arecommitting to pray for and engage with at their spiritual level. **Identify a few names for each circle and write them below.**

UNBELIEVERS
Those that don't know Jesus.
(at least 3 people)

NEWER BELIEVERS
Those you are actively discipling to go deeper in their walk with Jesus.
(at least 2 people)

ACCOUNTABILITY
A like-minded disciple maker for encouragement
(at least 1 person)

LIKE JESUS

LEARN MORE / DOWNLOAD THE APP:
LikeJesus.church

BUILDING A MOVEMENT OF MULTIPLICATION, LIKE JESUS DID.

—

A NEW CHURCH-WIDE RESOURCE BY DR. DANN SPADER TO HELP YOUR CHURCH OR MINISTRY CREATE A CULTURE OF DISCIPLE-MAKING.

Like Jesus contains four unique modules; one for your leadership team and three congregational modules that cover *The Mission of Jesus*, *The Model of Jesus* and *The Methods of Jesus*. Designed to be preached from the pulpit with small group study and discussion, each module includes sermon graphics, outlines, videos, logos as well as custom dashboards to track disciple-making engagement.

In addition, the Like Jesus app includes:

- ✓ DISCIPLE-MAKING ASSESSMENT
- 💬 SMALL GROUP ENGAGEMENT
- 📱 CHURCH APP INTEGRATION
- 📖 FULL E-BOOKS
- ▶ VIDEO CONTENT
- ❤ CIRCLE OF CONCERN

*The **Like Jesus app** is versatile and has a web portal that can be implemented into your current church app platform as well as a stand-alone app for iOS and Android.*

LEADERSHIP   MISSION   MODEL   METHODS

LIKE JESUS

"WHOEVER CLAIMS TO LIVE IN HIM MUST LIVE AS JESUS DID."
1 JOHN 2:6

🔹 LikeJesus.church

THE LIKE JESUS APP

—

The Like Jesus app was designed to both enhance the Like Jesus resource as well as help you, your church, ministry or small group: go deeper, provide robust disciple-making content, and add real-time metrics and feedback digitally. The app provides book and video content, interaction & engagement, church and personal assessments & key metrics to encourage disciple-making.

The app can be accessed via desktop (www.likejesus.church) as well as a stand-alone app for iOS and Android.

LEARN MORE:

 LikeJesus.church

CREATING A CULTURE OF DISCIPLE-MAKING,
LIKE JESUS DID.

Our Pathway for equipping leaders in relational disciple-making is as simple as BE ● BUILD ● BEGIN.

BE A DISCIPLE MAKER
Before seeing disciple-making fruit in our ministries, first we must personally BE a disciple-maker. We can't effectively lead people toward disciple-making if we're not living a disciple-making lifestyle.

BUILD A DISCIPLE-MAKING MINISTRY
If we want to BUILD a disciple-making ministry, it's critical that we use the proper blueprint and look at Jesus as our model.

BEGIN A DISCIPLE-MAKING MOVEMENT
Jesus began a movement 2000 years ago, and He has invited us to BEGIN movements right where we are... making and multiplying disciples from here to the ends of the earth.

Dr. Dann Spader is the founder of Sonlife, a disciple-making training organization whose mission is *"to equip leaders in relational disciple-making according to the Son's life."*

For free resources to fuel your disciple-making efforts, visit Sonlife.com

Be.
BUILD.
BEGIN.

Strategy
SEMINAR

MAKING AND MULTIPLYING
DISCIPLES AS JESUS DID ✕

How did the message of the gospel saturate the ancient
world, from Jerusalem to Rome, in less than 30 years without
planes, trains, or Twitter? It spread from person to person as
disciples were made and multiplied. As a result, entire regions were
saturated with the good news of Jesus as the mandate and mission
of Jesus to "go and make disciples of all nations" was being fulfilled.

We are convinced that by using the same strategy that Jesus modeled and
the early church employed, we can witness the good news of Jesus saturating
our cities, transforming our communities.

Sonlife's **Strategy Seminar** is an in-depth look at the Model, Mission, Motive, Method,
and Movement of Jesus.

For more information about hosting this 8 hour training event, visit Sonlife.com or call
(971) 340-4675